P9-APQ-618

Humans aren't perfect, and many stumble and fall. But *Close Calls* is filled with loving, practical advice that reminds us that humans are willing and eager to reach back and help others avoid destruction—find their way around the landmines. It will help you avoid the danger of complacency and, even better gives you the step-by-step path to protect your love, your marriage, your family, your dignity and your integrity.

—**Diane Sollee**
Founder and Director
Smart Marriages
Washington, DC

Ministering in a large church, I have seen where the similar interests and gifts that volunteers bring to service for Jesus often put spouses from different marriages on the same ministry team. These ministry friendships can easily become too personal over time and *Close Calls* addresses how to protect both the marriages and the ministry. As men and women interact more together at work, in the gym, in recreation, their children's sports, etc., attractions often naturally surface that can highlight unmet needs in the individual. Rather than deny their existence, *Close Calls,* drawing upon the difficult experiences of those who misused this attraction, provides direction on how to use these experiences to enrich your marriage.

—**Bob Baker**, MDiv., MFT
Chief of Staff
Saddleback Church
Mission Viejo, CA

CLOSE CALLS

What ADULTERERS Want
You to Know about
Protecting Your MARRIAGE

DAVE CARDER

NORTHFIELD PUBLISHING

CHICAGO

© 2008 by
DAVE CARDER

All rights reserved. No part of this book may be reproduced in any form without permission in writing from the publisher, except in the case of brief quotations embodied in critical articles or reviews.

Note: Some of the material in chapters 5, 6, and 9 first appeared in *Torn Asunder*, Moody Publishers, © 1992, 1995 by Dave Carder with Duncan Jaenicke and in *Torn Asunder Workbook*, Moody Publishers, © 2001 by Dave Carder.

Charts may be reproduced for ease in completing the exercises and activities in this book. No further copying is authorized.

Interior Design: Ragont Design
Cover Design: Kirk DouPonce, DogEared Design
(www.DogEaredDesign.com)

Library of Congress Cataloging-in-Publication Data

Carder, David.
  Close calls: what adulterers want you to know about protecting your marriage / by Dave Carder.
      p. cm.
  Includes bibliographical references.
  ISBN-13: 978-0-8024-4211-6
  ISBN-10: 0-8024-4211-0
  1. Adultery. 2. Marriage — Psychological aspects. I. Title.

HQ806.C315 2008
646.7'8 — dc22
                                              2007045975

We hope you enjoy this book from Northfield Publishing. Our goal is to provide high-quality, thought-provoking books and products that connect truth to your real needs and challenges. For more information on other books and products written and produced from a biblical perspective, go to www.moodypublishers.com or write to:

Northfield Publishing
215 West Locust Street
Chicago, IL 60610

3 5 7 9 10 8 6 4

Printed in the United States of America

To Ronnie, my spouse of forty-plus years —
the playful one in our relationship —
who taught me how to have fun and
who continues to make me look forward
to coming home at night!

CONTENTS

A special thanks to Jenni Key, member, board of directors, Evangelical Free Church of America, and director of communications, First Evangelical Free Church of Fullerton, who first heard me present this material in Thailand and who, on a hot, and sweaty, non-air conditioned trip back to the Bangkok Airport, said she would edit this book if I would just write it. You are a marriage lover, you believed in this material, and you hounded me until I finally wrote it.

GETTING STARTED:
A Note from the Author

I started listening to stories of adultery thirty years ago, and what you are going to read is what men and women who have committed adultery have taught me. Most of the people I've counseled in their recovery after adultery had thought they would be immune to having an affair. Few would have thought they were susceptible not only to falling into the arms of someone they weren't married to, but would not even have thought it possible that they could come close!

Close Calls is the result of years of listening to people who did just that. When I share what I've learned with couples attempting to recover from an affair, the standard response is, "I wish we had known this before. . . ."

Well, now you can learn what they wish they had known before they experienced the heartache of an affair. You can recognize when you may be heading toward or having a close call and pull back before you can't stop yourself.

DEVELOPMENT OF CLOSE CALLS

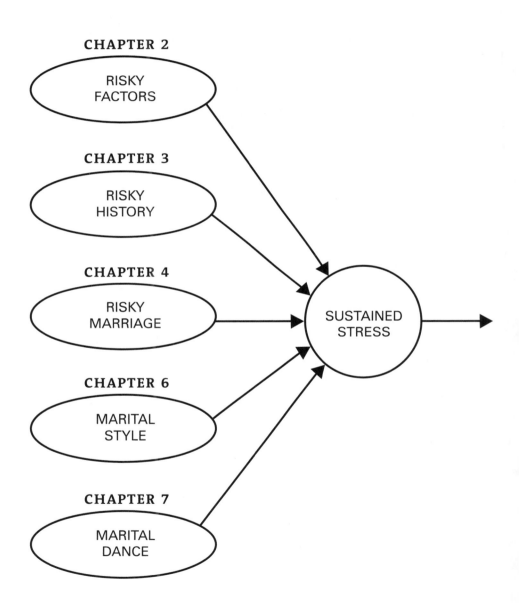

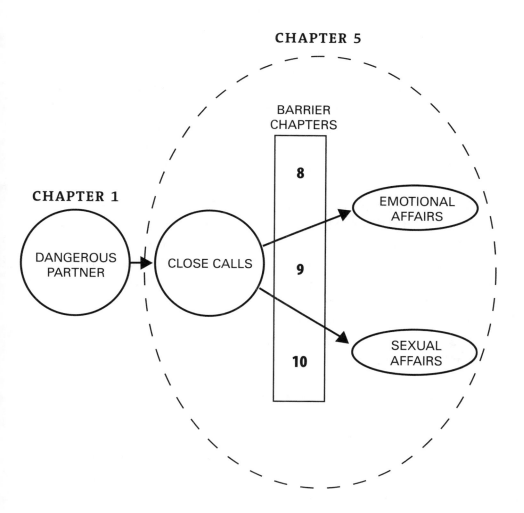

The material in this book will not only help you be more alert to a close call—it will strengthen your marriage. The two of you will remember what you first saw in each other and why you decided to choose each other as marriage partners.

You and your spouse will discover what kind of person might fit each of your dangerous partner profiles, you'll review your history as a couple, and you'll learn to recognize the high-risk factors each of you bring to the table. You will find out how to recognize those high-risk seasons we all pass through and be vigilant in spotting how these times are affecting you.

You'll notice themes that recur in accounts from people who did fall into having extramarital affairs and greatly damaged—or destroyed—their marriage. Learn from them so you can avoid doing the same thing.

Finally, this book will also make you aware of how close you may have come to getting involved with another individual in the past. You'll learn that an affair needs certain components to thrive, and you'll see how your close call *didn't* have all the components, and therefore *did not* result in an affair. That you even had a close call might startle you! Bad experiences are often created when people are not aware of their history. In this culture, more people than you might realize have close calls, and you might only recognize the close call for what it was when you look back on it. The better prepared you are, the better the outcome will be when the future relationship starts to develop an inappropriate level of attraction.

Some of you are already thinking, *I'm not sure I want to read this book.* I understand. I am sure it sounds intimidating, but here is the encouragement: If you (or better yet, you and your spouse) tackle the material presented here . . .

- you will finish it feeling closer to each other than you have ever felt;

- you will talk about subject matter you never dreamed you would find yourself discussing;
- you will understand your spouse at an entirely new level that will carry the two of you through your future transitions;
- you will find a whole new sense of safety to talk about "dangerous" information; and
- you will love the way that you can make sense out of experiences that you never fully understood prior to this discussion.

Throughout the book, you'll find interesting things to discuss, most of which you probably never had given a lot of thought to before. To enhance your thoughts and discussions, check out the appendix at the back of the book. You'll find plenty of descriptive words to capture just that right message, and you'll also find some guidelines to good communication and conflict resolution.

COULD THIS BE YOU?

Over the years I have heard hundreds of stories from couples struggling with threats to their marriage, ranging from emotionally charged friendships to sexual addiction.

All of these inappropriate relationships started with a close call encounter that the individual did not turn from and in some cases actually cultivated. All of the outcomes were horribly painful. You will feel that as you read these stories. These accounts have not been solicited and are told to you as they were told to me. Most are unedited e-mails that I have used with permission.

There are no conclusions in many of them because these stories are written by people engulfed in their chaos. Actually, some are written after the fact. The outcome still lies in the future for most of these folks, and all their energy is focused on just staying afloat in their current struggle. They are desperate, pouring out their hearts to anyone who will listen, and they agreed to let me share their stories with the hope that it might protect you and your spouse in the future.

Both the writers of those e-mails and I want you to get maximum benefit from these stories, so prior to each one, I will call attention to certain components that relate to the content of close calls. This is the same learning process that I have gone through for thirty years—listening to the stories of marriages currently caught in adultery. This is the part of every adulterous story that is rarely portrayed in the media but is always a big part of real life.

You will find these stories at the end of each chapter under the heading: "Could This Be You?"

SECTION 1:

Is a Close Call Stalking You?

DEVELOPMENT OF CLOSE CALLS

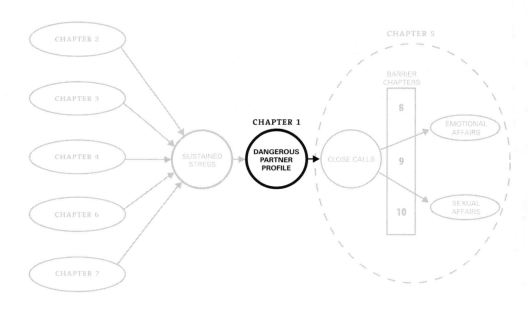

1 RISKY ATTRACTIONS:
Do You Know One?

CARMEN

Carmen put away her pregnancy test again with a heavy heart. For months now she had been going through this process after her monthly cycle. If she didn't get pregnant shortly, she and Ted knew they would have to get serious about starting infertility treatments. Both of them dreaded it, although Ted wasn't losing any sleep over it. He seemed to go through life with the "easy come/easy go" attitude that Carmen envied.

This trait was definitely what attracted her to him in the first place. Her own dad was a hard-driving executive, rarely home, who had left the entire child rearing responsibilities for her and her sister to their mother. Eventually they divorced; he married a much younger coworker and started another family in another state.

Carmen remembered thinking to herself at an early

age that when she started looking for a husband she wanted someone who was more laid-back and easygoing. Sure, she had to take more of the leadership in the home and she had to make more decisions, and at times she even felt more like Ted's mother than an adult partner, but overall she was happy.

Arriving at work a little late one day, she passed her boss's office. Mr. Caldwell looked up, smiled, and waved as she walked by. She felt like a spectacle at work. Everybody knew how much she wanted to have a baby, and she felt as if everybody knew when she took another pregnancy test. She had been back at her desk just a short while when she suddenly became aware that Mr. Caldwell was standing next to her. He asked how things were going, initiating what turned into a long conversation. He was old enough to be her father, was balding, and had a little paunch. He wasn't trim and good-looking like Ted, but he seemed so caring and was easy to confide in. He said he even had a daughter her age who was in the same predicament.

His concern was so very comforting. *No wonder all the girls in the office like him so much,* she thought as he patted her on the shoulder and reassured her that things were going to get better. Over the next few months his fatherly concern continued. At times Carmen felt he was more like a counselor than a boss. She knew he was on his third marriage and was disappointed to have gotten stuck in this midlevel management job, but for her and the other young women he was a perfect fatherboss.

Through the ensuing months, Carmen found herself confiding more and more in Mr. Caldwell. She knew Ted was beginning to have a harder time with the infertility as well, and she just couldn't dump all her feelings on him when he was struggling so much too.

One night Mr. Caldwell asked her to stay late to finish a project. That evening they started talking, and as usual, the conversation turned toward her struggle to get pregnant. She started crying and he held her while she cried on his shoulder. Nothing more happened for a while, and Carmen considered the encounter a show of his fatherly comfort.

In the meantime, she and Ted were becoming more frustrated with each other. All romance was gone from the marriage, and all their energies were focused on one thing: producing a baby.

Finally, pregnancy was achieved and Carmen and Ted could hardly contain their joy. Their family and friends and coworkers rejoiced with their happy announcement. But sadly, Carmen miscarried in the second month.

Carmen took a few days off work, and Mr. Caldwell called her at home to see how she was doing. You can figure out where this is going, can't you? They talked for three hours. Carmen didn't realize she'd been engaging in a close call for months, and that this lengthy, intimate phone conversation was about to tip the relationship one way or the other. It eventually led to an affair that Ted had the hardest time forgiving. He could never understand why his young and beautiful wife would get involved with a "fat old man" who was twice her age.

How indeed could she? Let's explore why this close call happened. Perhaps if Carmen had recognized Mr. Caldwell as a profile of her dangerous partner, this close call would have ended as a close call—and not ruined a marriage.

THE DANGEROUS PARTNER PROFILE

Mr. Caldwell might not have looked like a potential dangerous partner, but for Carmen he was. Not every man holds the same attraction for every woman and vice versa. But with the dangerous partner profile person, the attraction is immediate and passionate. As we began to explore this concept, remember the following concerns:

- The reason you didn't marry someone like your dangerous partner profile person is because you knew intuitively that such a person would not be good for you in the long run.
- Your spouse might be very different from your dangerous partner profile person, but that doesn't mean that he/she is less attractive to you.
- Dangerous partner profile persons are composites of those individuals who appear to meet all of the deficits you bring to your marriage.
- The dangerous partner profile person often defies all of your training, culture, common sense, and values. There is often no apparent logic in the close call or even in the affair with a dangerous partner profile person.
- A dangerous partner profile is lurking in the subconscious of all of us and remains there as a powerful secret until a couple is willing to talk out the composite images that reside in each of them.

Let me share a story about "the bits and pieces," or "composite concept" I mentioned above.

Sally was married to an engineer. She was impressed very early in their dating experience with the thoughtful and calm demeanor Trent displayed. She had grown up in an alcoholic family that was the exact opposite: chaotic, verbally hurtful, full of drama. Every day held unexpected experiences.

However, after marriage to Trent for several years, she found herself yearning for some excitement. Life looked great on the outside, but actually she was bored. As her dissatisfaction continued to grow, she started looking for something to be involved with and eventually started volunteering to provide ESL services to adults from the local Hispanic community.

Over time, she became quite committed to several young men who were fairly recent arrivals from Latin America. She became very involved with their progress and found herself being not only their language teacher, but also their cheerleader, job trainer, surrogate mother. She started bringing them food, coupons, and money that she collected from friends.

Eventually, her favorite in the group got a job and was able to buy a motorcycle. He came by and wanted to take her for a ride. She accepted. Within weeks, they were taking brief secret trips, and this close call was too close to being inappropriate. She knew this was "crazy-making" behavior, called it off, and told Trent.

In talking with Trent, Sally realized that "the bits and pieces" she needed in her marriage were spontaneous getaways, surprises, unexpected, unplanned times together. Trent was the ultimate planner, and his predictability had often drained the excitement from an experience. As they talked about this issue, they both realized they could make their marriage better and more interesting, and they became excited as they saw a shift coming in their relationship.

This is exactly how understanding the dangerous partner profile can make an already good marriage better.

Take some time with your spouse to talk about this concept to understand what kind of person is a dangerous partner for each of you. Making this a conversational topic will likely require grace on both of your parts. Your spouse might even have a better idea of what some of these attractive components are for you than you do! Give a listening ear and consider strongly what he or she observes. Look at the chart below. You'll see a number of areas that cause attraction to a dangerous partner. Keep the page marked; you'll go back to it as you read through the chapter.

PROFILE OF YOUR DANGEROUS PARTNER	
Developmental lags	
Personality style	
Hobbies/Interests	
Attachment pattern	
Family of origin	
Marital void	
Pursuit pattern	
Internal age	

Developmental Lags

Alcoholism or other addictions, chronic debilitating illness, a disability in the family, an absent parent, parental expectations, having too much responsibility, even patterns and values, can all lead to a child aging too quickly. Entire sections of life are skipped. Those missed developmental periods often surface later in life with close call attractions and are definitely a part of the attraction of the dangerous partner.

For instance, a child whose parents or culture put excessive demands on their academic achievement to the exclusion of adolescent dating practices will often revert to those practices as an adult. In fact, entire cultures tolerate males continuing to "date" though married, and wives are expected to look the other way.

Early adolescent drug and alcohol use can also create this kind of developmental lag in an individual.

Not only does developmental lag occur in individuals, it can also occur in relationships. When I teach premarital classes, I often say, "Your relationship is only as old as it is nonsexual. The relationship stops growing once it becomes sexual, because the physical aspect will become the primary focus. It is the sexual *tension* in a dating relationship that drives you to get to know the other person and that keeps you exploring the difficult subjects that are necessary to establish a long-term, well-matched experience."

Buck and Jill met in a college class and at first had a lot to talk about. Their physical relationship didn't go beyond hand holding, hugging, or kissing, but after about three months, they began sleeping together. Their relationship didn't deepen much beyond that point, as their focus became more on making love than on learning more about each other. In other words, regardless of how long a couple has dated, if their relationship became sexual within three months of the onset of dating, they have a three-month-old relationship. It is more fun to have sex than it is to discuss difficult subjects. Besides (or so the couple thinks), *We want to enjoy our time together, so why rock the boat and create unnecessary conflict?* To which I say—better now than later!

Consider and write down what development lags you notice in your life. You'll soon see how these could attract you to a dangerous partner.

Personality Style

Very often, an individual marries a spouse with a personality very different from that of the dangerous partner profile. Intuitively, they knew that in the long run their spouse's personality style would be best for them. But the dangerous partner's personality style still holds intrigue for the individual.

23

Many times this dangerous partner's personality profile mimics that of a significant person from your adolescent history. It can be someone you were personally acquainted with, like an old girlfriend or boyfriend you broke up with; someone you knew from a distance, like a high school or college athlete; or, as is very often the case, someone you never knew, but always dreamed of being with, e.g., a famous teen idol, the star in a movie that you have never forgotten, and so on.

On the other hand, this personality can also reflect a pattern that you have or have not experienced in a close relationship. An illustration might be the woman who stays safe and marries a tradesman like her father, but always wished she could have married an educated, well-traveled, college professor. A young boy lives in chaos with an overwhelmed, very busy, professionally trained single mom. In reaction to what he never had, he decides to marry a woman with a high school education who has no interest in a career and who will be content to be a stay-at-home wife. However, he soon becomes bored with her, and the thought of an exciting, outgoing, independent woman suddenly takes on new appeal.

Whatever the pattern, it is important to remember that invariably the dangerous partner personality is going to be different from that of your spouse. That's what makes them attractive. That's what creates the intrigue.

But just having a different personality is insufficient to create a close call without the other variables in this profile.

Write your own personality style on the chart. You may also write about a personality style to whom you are attracted.

Hobbies and Interests

There often appears to be an automatic connection with an individual who shares interests similar to yours. You immediately have something to talk about, and often this conversation is of little interest to your spouse. You admire their involvement in this activity and they automatically have a higher value in your estimation. Sometimes you have a desire to be more involved in this hobby or activity, but the lack of interest on the part of your spouse inhibits this involvement. The emotional reaction is often a disappointment in the spouse and even anger that you can't be involved to the degree that you would like without upsetting the marriage. Even if you are satisfied with the amount of spousal support you receive, hobbies and interests are still part of the dangerous partner profile.

What are your hobbies and interests? What would you like to share with someone else? To get you thinking: You'll often have an automatic connection with an individual who shares interests similar to yours. . . . You admire his involvement in this activity and he automatically . . . Sometimes you desire to be more involved . . . but you're inhibited by your husband's lack of interest. . . . You wish your wife could enjoy . . .

Attachment Pattern

An attachment pattern is one of the many processes through which spouses are initially attracted to each other. They don't always discuss it; in fact, they might not even be aware of these attractions right away, but it refers to that cluster of behaviors that make one individual particularly appealing to the other. Yet men and women I've spoken with tell me that they often find themselves attracted to relationships that have an attraction pattern opposite that of their marriage. For example, in marriage a spouse will sometimes select a partner who is independent, strong, self-contained, and competent. But the close call comes as they are attracted to someone who is clingy, needy, desperate to be rescued, and lost.

In the marriage, some spouses want to be in charge of everything. But when they succumb to an affair, they want to be taken care of. In the marriage, they are dependent. In the affair, they want to be independent. In the marriage, they rarely initiate sex.

In the affair, they initiate all the lovemaking. This is often why forgiveness is so difficult on the part of the faithful spouse. They may have wanted their spouse to share in the load they were carrying, but that didn't happen until their spouse was involved with someone else.

Why does this opposite attraction pattern seem almost universal in affairs? I think it has to do with what I've come to call the Moon-Earth Syndrome. When you look at the moon at night from planet Earth, you always see the same "face" or view of the moon. You might see a new quarter, the third quarter, a new moon, or even a full moon, but you always see the same "face." No one ever sees the other side of the moon unless they travel to space.

That is the way most marriages function. Over time, the spouses come to face each other the same way, day in and day out. You come to settle for what you "see." It develops predictability, trust, efficiency, and effectiveness. But what you "see" is just half of what there is to know about your spouse. To settle for this produces boredom, dullness, and even a feeling of being taken for granted—that is, until another person, the "dangerous partner," comes along and touches them on the "dark side." Not the evil side, just the unexplored side that the spouse is not interested in exploring, doesn't value, or doesn't have time to take a look at.

What sort of attachment pattern do you see yourself looking for?

Family of Origin Deficits

Through the years of talking with adulterers, I have long been amazed at how many close call attractions happen when the "dangerous partner" stirs up long forgotten family of origin deficits. Here is the little girl looking for the father lost through divorce, the little boy longing for the emotional nurturance of a warm and loving mother. Here is the child looking for someone to protect them, to provide for them, to see them as special, to admire and look up to them, to care for and understand them in ways that they never experienced in their family of origin. (We'll talk about family of origin in more detail in chapter 2.)

The opposite can also be true in some circumstances. Some children have these needs met in their family of origin but, for a variety of reasons, these basic emotional needs are not met in their marriage. This marital void is the subject of the next part of the "dangerous partner." (Note on the chart which family of origin deficits you might be tempted to make up with someone other than your spouse.)

Marital Voids

If you believe, like I do, that most marriages get in trouble because the spouses stop doing what they do best, then this section will be especially helpful to you. I believe that a spouse's failure to nurture the other spouse, in ways that he or she desires, can make the spouse vulnerable to an individual with their particular "dangerous partner profile." This marital void has two components: emotional and activity.

1. Emotional Component

When you first started dating, nobody told you that you had to affirm, admire, and be affectionate with the person you were dating. You did that automatically because you liked her. Nobody was making you date this particular individual. You even married her because you liked her, and you continued to treat her as a special person, uniquely different from all your other friends — for a while.

There are five special treatments, readily apparent when you are infatuated with each other. Many couples have stopped practicing them even though this is what they used to do best: *accommodate, admire, adore, affirm*, and show *affection* for each other. These are the kinds of attitudes and expressions that drew you to each other. They are also exactly what the "dangerous partner" will utilize to create a close call and to attract your spouse into an illicit relationship. The language of attraction becomes the language of seduction.

When I am counseling a couple in postadultery recovery, the spouse who has been unfaithful often weeps when I mention these. Why? Because we all like to hang out with folks who would rather be with us more than anything or anyone else (accommodation). We all like to converse with those who look up to us (adoration), respect what we do and who we are (admiration), tell us what they think is so great about us (affirmation), and take the time to show us these things in ways we enjoy (affection). This is what you used to do best. However, many couples have come to settle for less of these practices than either spouse has wanted. Many of us are starved for this kind of nurturance.

2. Activity Component

There are deficits that occur in every marriage (we will explore this more later on). Here I want to emphasize the one deficit that is universal to marriages that experience adultery: the loss of fun. Most couples just stop having fun together. They don't spend money on their marriage. They have stopped building memories between just the two of them. They are consumed with making it through the day, to the end of the month, all the while hoping for something better next year.

In order to have time for yourselves, you have to steal it from your children. Yes, you read that right! Children are born narcissistic and egocentric, and they will take all the time, all the energy, all the money you have and still not be satisfied. You can build great family memories with your children all there in one place (we have four adult children and five grandchildren), but you can only build a personal relationship between the two of you when you are alone with each other. Having fun together will help prevent the close call of finding fun with someone else!

Are there things you've stopped doing? Are these voids that someone else might come along and fill?

Pursuit Pattern

This is the pattern of attention that you are most vulnerable to. Does it make you uncomfortable when someone of the opposite sex says nice things to you, or are you so starved for their affirmation that you become weak in the knees? Are you susceptible when somebody comes after you? Or do you have to go after them to feel vulnerable? Do you want to be caught, or do you want to give chase? Some folks become afraid and run when faced with someone coming on to them. Others will take the bait and love just to see if they can conquer the individual who appears to be fleeing but is really just fluttering. Do you run when tempted, or do you have a tendency to try to manage the temptation?

Note your tendencies in this area.

Internal Age

Did you know that every person has an internal, developmental age as well as an external, chronological age? Rarely do the two match perfectly across the life span. Any number of circumstances, individuals, or environments can trigger either a regression or a rapid advancement in internal age.

Often certain individuals can make each of us feel incompetent or stupid, or on the other hand, superior or attractive. Our roles and environments can influence our feelings of our internal age. For instance, the smaller an individual's role in life, usually the younger they feel. Sometimes we have a yearning to go back to an "idealized age," a time when everything seemed perfect, with very little or no responsibility.

Others of us are so worn out from caring for so many for so long that we yearn for somebody to take care of us. All of these factors illustrate internal age. Almost always, the partner in an affair matches the unfaithful spouse's internal age. The gaps between internal and chronological age within each spouse and between spouses can create close calls in a marriage.

How old are you on the inside? Most of us have not spent a lot of time thinking about or discussing this concept with anyone. So to help you identify your internal age, look at the Internal Age chart. Each of you jot down your answers first, then sit down and discuss them before going on. You'll enjoy this activity!

LOOKING AT YOUR INTERNAL AGE

Did you know that you have an internal age that, at various times, might be at odds with your chronological age? Here are some questions to jog your thinking about your internal age.

How old do I feel today? Why?

What is the idealized age I would like to return to if I could? Why?

What was the biggest gap, and at what age did it occur between my internal age and my chronological age? Why is that?

Did I ever "get stuck" internally and stop growing? Why? What happened?

What makes me feel older on the inside than what I am chronologically?

How old was I on the inside when I met my spouse? Why? What made me feel that way?

Have I continued to grow and develop like I should? Why or why not?

How do people in authority make me feel on the inside? Why?

When I'm around my parents, how old do I feel? Why?

What person makes me feel older/younger? Why?

How has my current role in life influenced my internal age?

SUMMARY OF THE DANGEROUS PARTNER PROFILE

- What is the profile of your dangerous partner? Are you surprised?
- Is it shocking to see it written out?
- Does it bring to mind close calls that you've had in the past with individuals who match this profile?
- Has it been threatening to your spouse as you discussed this?
- Are you currently in close proximity to any individuals that match this profile?
- How do you feel about your spouse's dangerous partner profile?
- Are you surprised, or did you know that this vulnerability had been there for a long time?

I hope the two of you have had a good time talking about this issue. Remember, just about everybody is tempted in this culture. Nearly everyone has close calls, unless you're dead or in denial.

That brings up another part of this discussion. Are you willing to make the following commitment to each other? Should either of you feel attracted to another individual, and before the attraction has a chance to develop

- you will tell each other;
- you will promise to listen to the other without becoming angry;
- together you will explore ways to disarm the attraction;
- you will thank your spouse for his or her courage in bringing this up.

Activation Requirements

Okay, now your spouse is concerned that you'll go to work tomorrow and cross paths with a dangerous partner profile person! If you do, is an affair inevitable? Not so fast. This dangerous individual is only energized when several other variables are in place. Take a look:

High-Risk Factors + Stressors + Dangerous Partner = Close Call

In order for the dangerous partner profile person to be energized in your life or your spouse's life, all three of these clusters need to be in place. In the following chapters, we'll discuss other components shown in the mix: high-risk factors (includes marital style) and circumstantial stressors.

COULD THIS BE YOU?

I chose to put this story first because it is one of the more thorough presentations of the sequences involved in a close call that eventually leads to adultery. As you begin reading, you'll notice that Sam was not looking for someone else. He was minding his own business, but he was in the midst of several stressors in his marriage when, out of his past, up pops his close call. Notice how he fails to recognize the danger until he looks back on the experience. Then, when he's caught, he tries to keep the illicit relationship going at all costs! These are the enticing earmarks of a close call. Read Sam's story:

"I am at my wit's end looking for help. I cannot watch my
family go down the drain without trying every possible option. First and foremost, this is all my fault. I am not blaming anyone for this mess but myself. Some of this may sound like I'm making excuses, but I am not.

"I am a forty-six-year-old physician. Rachel is a

forty-six-year-old executive turned stay-at-home mom. It is my first marriage; Rachel had a short marriage in her twenties that ended in divorce. When we married, we were very much in love; not only that, but both of us thought that we were a perfect match. We have similar values, interests, and aspirations. She is more passionate than I am, and I am convinced that she 'feels' her emotions (good and bad ones) more than I feel mine. I am an introvert; she is an extrovert. Until I committed the unthinkable, I have always been a straight arrow who did what was right.

"I grew up in a two-parent family that seemed normal enough, except my dad and mom didn't really have any common interests and, to this day, don't do much together. I never felt unloved, although my dad was not verbally expressive.

"Rachel was adopted as a baby and reared by her grandmother after her biological parents essentially abandoned her to her grandmother. To further confuse Rachel, her parents did rear her siblings, sometimes living as close as the house next door. She knew they were her parents and siblings, but she never knew why she wasn't with them. As you might imagine, this was very difficult on her as a child, and the effects linger with her to this day. She has always had a difficult time believing that anyone (including me) loved and wanted her.

"Rachel and I both grew up going to church. In my midlife, primarily by devoting excessive time and energy to my practice, I am ashamed that I let my spiritual and marital life deteriorate. Although I attend church, for several years prior to this crisis I had essentially been just filling a seat there. And while our marriage hasn't been terrible, it has been sick for several years. Unfortunately, much of this I was unable to see before my life came crashing down last year. Rachel has been much stronger spiritually than I, and until the affair, she also put more effort into our marriage.

"Twenty some years ago, when I was in college, I was engaged to another woman. However, I decided that I did not want to marry her, and I broke the engagement—but strange as it seems, I continued to date the woman off and on for over a year after that before it finally ended. The woman later married another man, and after cheating on him several years later, divorced and married another. Even while she was married to her first husband, every couple of years or so, she would call me 'just to talk.' I guess I was too stupid to see how dangerous this behavior was.

"I hadn't heard from her in seven or eight years when, out of the blue, she stopped by my office to visit about five years ago. We talked some about old times, and she left. She knew I was married, and I should have told her then and there not to contact me, but I didn't. After that, maybe once a year or so, she would call me, talk a little while, and then I wouldn't hear from her again for another year or so.

"I hadn't heard from her for several years when she showed up at a medical conference I was attending. She came looking for me. We talked awhile and she left. Two days later, she came back, bringing with her photos and mementos of our days in college when we were engaged. Like I said, my marriage had been sick in recent years, and by the end of our conversation, my head was spinning with some of the most stupid thoughts of my life.

"Shortly afterward, in the beginning of a series of the most regrettable things I have ever done, I called her to tell her that I would be at another conference later that month. She came by, we sat in the car and talked, and eventually, at her invitation, kissed. Afterward, she started calling me three or four times a week. This continued for a month or so, until we decided to meet to talk in person. At this point, my head was totally screwed up. I can't understand how a normally rational person like me could let myself get involved in such a thing.

"Unfortunately, I arranged for us to meet at a hotel. She brought more photos, mementos, and old letters I had written over twenty years before. Over the next several months, I became emotionally and sexually entangled with her. During this time I did, said, and even wrote things that I now know are not true.

"As you might expect, any problem that I already had with my marriage and family was magnified a thousand times because of this affair. That in turn made the affair look more attractive in a continuing vicious cycle of destruction. My wife knew something was wrong, but she could not believe that I would ever betray her in this way. I even have a hard time believing that I did this to Rachel and my family.

"Late during this fiasco, I began to think that this wasn't such a good idea, couldn't possibly work out, and that I didn't have any genuine feelings for the other woman. But when her husband found out and made her stop, I did some of the most irrational, stupid things I've ever done trying to continue seeing her. I had ruined the already-damaged relationship with Rachel, the love of my life, and I just panicked, trying to continue what only days before I had been trying to figure out how to get out of.

"Finally, the other woman's husband called Rachel, telling her of the betrayal. Regardless of how many problems we had, she had totally trusted me to honor my wedding vows. I cannot tell you how much I regret what I have done to Rachel and to us as a couple.

"Which brings me to why I have contacted you. Six months later, we are on the verge of separation and divorce. Rachel just cannot get over what I have done to her. We have been to counselors, both individually and, only a little, together. I have treated her like a queen for six months, written her love letters, virtually abandoned my practice to spend time with her—everything I can possibly think of. She says she can forgive me as a person, but that she can't as a husband. She says that I 'threw her away' for another woman; that she can never trust me again; that she doesn't love me, like me, or respect me, that she will never feel special to me again; that I killed her love for me; that she would rather I had killed her than have done what I did. Just today, she has asked me to move out of the house. She has even said that I love this other woman and one day will go back to her.

"Nothing can be further from the truth. I love my wife and family, and the thought of losing them is too much to bear. We've prayed for help and guidance, but we just haven't made any progress. Over the past six months, she has fluctuated quite a bit, but always seems to come back to a literal rage of depression, bitterness, anger, and hurt. It has been hell, and it looks like it's going to explode."

DEVELOPMENT OF CLOSE CALLS

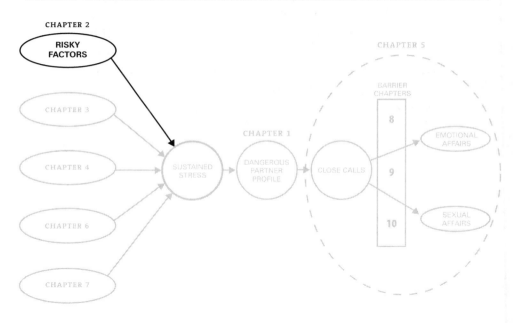

CHAPTER 2

RISKY FACTORS

CHAPTER 3

CHAPTER 4

CHAPTER 6

CHAPTER 7

SUSTAINED STRESS

CHAPTER 1

DANGEROUS PARTNER PROFILE

CLOSE CALLS

CHAPTER 5

BARRIER CHAPTERS

8

9

10

EMOTIONAL AFFAIRS

SEXUAL AFFAIRS

2 RISKY FACTORS:
What Are Yours?

JODY

Jody and Steve, both sobbing, married less than two years, sat in my office as Jody told the story of the close call that led to her illicit involvement with Dr. Morrison.

It seems that Jody's dad left the family when she was about four, the youngest of three girls. Mom was able to support the family adequately during the years the children were in the home, but, as with any single mother, her mom was always tired and often unable to meet all of the girls' emotional needs.

She did, however, teach them to become incredibly efficient and independent. They learned early on to pick up the slack, do what needed to be done to both help Mom and to keep the family running smoothly. As Mom put it, "I am even too tired to date." So the four of them worked hard to create their own special family.

The daughters were good students who valued education. All three graduated from college. Dad had never been in the picture a lot after he left with his girlfriend, moved to another state, and started another family.

None of the girls dated much, and when Jody entered a Christian university she was committed to her studies. She chose the nursing profession, excelled in both the classroom and the clinical work, and graduated with honors. In the summer prior to her senior year, she met Steve at the Christian camp where she was the nurse and he was a waterfront instructor. They hit it off immediately.

At the end of the summer both of them thought their relationship had potential, and with Steve's attendance at the nearby state university, they were able to date on a regular basis. After graduation they married. Soon Jody passed the boards and started work at a local hospital. Steve got the accounting job that was on the CPA track. Both appeared very happy.

At the hospital, Jody excelled in her nursing care. She was young, attractive, and smart, and was kind and supportive to patients and coworkers. It wasn't long before Dr. Morrison started making public comments at the nurse's station about the care she was showing his patients. Jody found herself glowing on the inside. For a man of Dr. Morrison's caliber to make comments like that was heady praise indeed.

If Jody had understood where she was at risk, she could have recognized Dr. Morrison's behavior and her reaction as a close call and kept the relationship impersonal. Instead, here's what happened:

Before long the other nurses started teasing Jody that Dr. Morrison was actually flirting with her. She denied it, saying he was a married man and she was newly married as well. He was just being friendly and appreciative. But she did find herself looking forward to the time that she knew he would be in the hospital making rounds.

Rather quickly over the next few months, their professional relationship escalated to having coffee and even lunch in the hospital cafeteria. Dr. Morrison was her father's age, she argued to herself, but all to no avail. She found herself soaking up his recognition, encouragement, and support. It awakened something deep inside her that she didn't even know existed.

Steve, meanwhile, was becoming increasingly busy during the final two months of the company's fiscal year. He often worked late through the evenings. Jody wasn't sure if she had mentioned that to Dr. Morrison, or if maybe one of the other nurses had said something to him, but he asked her out for supper one night. She knew she shouldn't go. She did not tell Steve. But she went.

Nothing happened. She had a glass of wine, a great meal, and a good time at a nice place, but that was just the beginning. Before long, Jody and Dr. Morrison started arriving at the restaurant in the same car, and he started taking her home. Soon she was inviting him in, and they became sexually involved.

She knew she needed to stop the relationship, but she couldn't. This highly respected older man was meeting needs in her life that her new husband, Steve, wasn't even aware of. The sex wasn't that great, but the rest of the evening together was delightful.

Finally, one of her nursing friends confronted her about having an affair with Dr. Morrison. She denied it, but she suddenly realized that it was apparent to everybody. She knew she had to stop it and told Dr. Morrison at their next dinner. He became demanding and told her she couldn't stop seeing him. He started pressuring her to meet him at hotels in the afternoon if she wouldn't have dinner with him. He even threatened to expose her, and she was suddenly terrified of losing her job.

Jody knew she needed help in getting out, and she knew she would have to tell Steve. Suddenly, what had been so delightful, what had met a deep emotional need in her life for a loving, older mentor male, had turned very ugly. She finally stopped the relationship, changed hospitals, and tried to save her marriage. But Steve just found it too hard to rebuild trust in his new wife. So much of their brief marital history had been corrupted by this illicit sexual relationship that he just couldn't recover. Twenty months after they married, they divorced.

HIGH-RISK FAMILY OF ORIGIN HISTORY

Jody's story illustrates just one of the several risk factors in a family of origin that can make an individual vulnerable to infidelity. When I share the following information with couples after adultery, the common response is, "That makes so much sense. Why didn't anybody tell us that when we got married?" So take a look at the concepts below and check off your own risk factors.

Family History of Infidelity

One doesn't have to work very long in the field of adultery recovery to begin to realize that infidelity runs in family trees. Infidelity can almost be a "given," because it is the universal temptation. Exactly how this behavior gets passed down to younger family members is still uncertain, but that this pattern exists should be treated as the norm. It is just not a common topic of conversation in most families, so children are often unaware of the family history of infidelity. Modeling is the most powerful behavioral determinant known to man. Even though the child may be too young to understand the dynamic going on in the family when adultery occurs, they nevertheless feel the tension, pain, and hostility that exists between the parents. Remember, Jody's father left the family when she was too young to understand that he most likely developed a relationship with another woman.

It might be this marital atmosphere that creates an injury

in a child that later surfaces in adulthood and makes the individual vulnerable to inappropriate affection and nurturance offered in a close call by someone outside the marriage.

Single Parent/Blended Family

Having taught divorce recovery and premarital/remarriage classes for years, I've observed that this family pattern struggles to provide the interactive nurturing that we all need and that can exist more easily in a two-parent nuclear family. Single-parent families, with a parent missing, have a much harder time trying to make up this deficit. Jody's family of her mother and sisters was a happy enough one, but missing male affirmation and affection was a deficit she might not have been aware of. The other difficulty is that it can take years of hard work to establish these kinds of relationships in even the best blended family systems.

Meanwhile, family members continue to mature, unaware of what they are not receiving. Individuals with these unmet childhood needs often select a spouse or even tolerate inappropriate spousal behavior, all under the guise of seeking what they have always wanted and have never had. This selection influence often results in disappointment with the chosen partner. Spouses are not designed to make up parental deficits. More often than not, engaged couples rarely think to address this issue.

Physically Abusive/Chronically Conflicted Family

It is common knowledge that most adult addictions have their roots in a family of origin atmosphere of anger and shame. That certainly is true of sexual addiction/compulsivity in males. Sex is very healing to men. Men who come out of angry families have often learned that sex is the primary way to reassure yourself that all is well. It is the need for a missing sense of well-being that partly drives the compulsive need for sex in young males who grow up in angry families.

43

It is helpful for wives to understand that sex is the best anti-depressant known to males. When men are anxious and depressed, or feel uneasy about their environment, they will often choose sex as their medication of choice. If that is not available in the marriage during the high-risk seasons (you'll read about these in chapter 3), or if the individual has used sex as a form of medication in adolescence, or seen a parent do so, then the risk is increased. Even in good marriages, husbands are often accused of viewing sexual relations as the answer to every difficulty!

There is a biochemical reason why males seek this sexual comfort in the midst of distress. They report the highest levels of oxytocin (the so-called bonding hormone) after sexual relations with their significant other. This spike does not occur in acts of masturbation or sexual interactions with prostitutes and strangers, but needing this reassurance can make men, with this risk factor vulnerable to a close call and inappropriate relationship. A common complaint, even among healthy marriages, is that often after marital conflict many husbands want to make love to their wives.

If sex occurs, they think all is well in the marriage while nothing might be further from the truth!

HIGH-RISK PERSONAL FACTORS

Sexual Molestation

A dismaying number of people report that they were sexually molested when they were minors.[1] Most authorities would tell you that anywhere from 25 to 40 percent of young women and approximately 20 percent of young males report having been sexually molested when they were minors. It is common knowledge that molested children often appear precocious and resort to promiscuous sexual behavior during adolescence and beyond. This is usually viewed as an attempt to work through the shame caused by their molestation experiences.

When shame and guilt feelings are attached to pleasant sexual experiences, it often creates ambivalence about spousal sexual activity or even an attitude that sex is bad. It is often difficult for the molested child to feel attractive as an adult and to enjoy the pleasant sexual passions that are part of a good marriage. Sex for this person can leave them feeling emotionally unsatisfied at best, and dirty and guilty at worst. Yet this need remains unfulfilled, and there can develop a "good sex"/"bad sex" split that makes the individual vulnerable to a sexual relationship with a "bad" person, i.e., someone other than their spouse.

After her third affair, Sara reported that she needed the reassurance that her seductiveness provided when one of her fellow workers succumbed to her flirtations. Molested as a child by an older half brother and an uncle, she could never enjoy sexual relations with her husband without recalling many of those terrible memories. However, when having the "bad" sexual relations with men she didn't love, she was able to experience everything that she wasn't able to experience in the marriage. It had nothing to do with her husband and everything to do with her history.

It is suspected that males underreport this experience due to many of their perpetrators being just slightly older babysitters, female cousins, half sisters, and other individuals well known by the family. Coupled with this is the tendency for males to focus on the pleasure of the experience versus the shame that young females often report.

Many times, mothers and other female family members discount the sexual impressionableness of the nine- and ten-year-old males in the home and dress inappropriately. When young boys are exposed to sexually arousing experiences at this age, they never forget them. Tom, at age six, went to live with his older sister who, though recently married, had just sent her husband off to a navy deployment. Base housing had no air conditioning, and they shared the only bed in the apartment. Due to the heat, she slept topless. Though nothing happened between the two of them, Tom reported that his curiosity over attempting to see women's breasts has been a lifelong struggle for him, and he never realized the source until we started looking at his history.

Adolescent Promiscuity

From the beginning, adulterers have talked about their adolescent sexual history. As a result, I have had a long-standing suspicion that, at some level, promiscuous adolescents would have a higher risk of adultery later in adulthood.

The question is: At what level of sexual activity in adolescence should an individual be considered promiscuous? In some studies, researchers label an individual "promiscuous" as someone who has had six or more sexual partners during adolescence (ages thirteen to twenty).

While I was talking with one such man who met this criterion, he made the comment, "You never forget the excitement of those sexual escapades!" It makes sense because adolescence is a time of heightened sensitivity in a number of different arenas. Cars, athletic experiences, girlfriends and boyfriends, and music, to name a few categories, always seem to be special in our memories. When life gets difficult, most of us would like to return to the simple and pleasant experiences of the way we remember our teenage years. That lure often leads to close calls and adultery.

Learning Disabilities and ADHD

Those with these diagnoses often report difficult childhoods. People are always yelling at them. No one ever seems pleased with their behavior. They're never quite good enough. They always seem to be in trouble. They can't ever seem to finish anything on time. Life is very difficult for them. People and even friends have a tendency to shun them. Authority figures see them as a nuisance, at best. They don't "wear well" in their environments and are often in trouble with bill collectors, the law, their family, and their bosses.

Those with high-risk personal histories are often singled out for therapists to see, doctors to medicate, and pastors to pray for. As a result, they have a high need for nurturance and reassurance. They are very vulnerable to anyone who will pay attention to them, listen to them, and support them. They are desperate for acceptance even while pretending that it is unnecessary. Saying or hearing "no" is difficult for them, and their poor impulse control is repeatedly getting them into trouble. They don't learn easily from their mistakes, and due to their desperate need for affection, they often find it difficult both to admit wrongdoing and to accept responsibility for their behavior.

COULD THIS BE YOU?

The following story highlights many of the family of origin risks that we talked about early in this chapter. Pay close attention to these factors, because in most cases, most of us would not think that these kinds of childhood deficits would still be having an impact on us as adults many years later. These deficits never go away, and though Wanda doesn't tell us exactly how the affair was an attempt to meet some of those needs, she does acknowledge that they were an influence in this close call attraction. Notice, too, the radical effort that Reuben had to take in order the break the attraction to the dangerous partner. Finally, as is often the case, notice how difficult it is for Wanda to manage her thoughts about this affair, even though it occurred thirty and forty years ago.

Here's Wanda's story in her own words:

"Reuben and I are both seventy-six years old. A year ago he finally confessed to me that he had been committing adultery for fifteen years with a secretary with whom he worked. We moved from one state to another at that time, but he still considered her to be a 'good friend' whom he called frequently and would meet with secretly when we made visits back there.

"From time to time during the years of his active involvement with her, I would become suspicious and inquire about his relationship, which was always vehemently denied. I had such faith in him and his integrity that I would believe him. We have always had a very active church life, and Reuben has a good knowledge of Scripture. One of the reasons I married him was because I felt he had an outstanding moral character.

"I love him deeply, and he claimed the reason he decided we should leave the state was because he knew he would lose me, and he wanted to spend the rest of his life with me. We did not consider divorce, and I forgave him immediately. We felt that we could recover and rebuild our marriage without outside counseling, using God's guidance and help.

"I did learn about your book *Torn Asunder* from the Focus on the Family Web site, and it was a great comfort to me to read your description concerning childhood thinking patterns infiltrating adult reality. In attempting to understand what could have caused Reuben to stray, and for such an extended time, I have tried to review all aspects of our relationship over the past fifty-plus years. Always my thoughts return to the baggage we brought to our marriage from our childhood.

"My father had a serious drinking problem, which had a very negative effect on his relationship with my mother. The trauma this created for me was relieved to some degree by my grandparents, who were wonderful counselors in this situation. I had someone who helped me work through my emotional situation during my childhood.

"On the other hand, Reuben's mother died from cancer when he was eight years old. After his father walked into the bedroom and told him his mother had died during the night, no one ever talked to him about the situation. His world had crumbled, and he had no one with whom to talk.

"His father remarried after nine months to a woman who was extremely self-centered, among many other negative traits. There was no overt love in the family and much subtle emotional abuse.

"In reviewing our relationship through all these years, there were many times when Reuben abused me emotionally — mainly verbally by unkind remarks — especially in public. We had an active sexual life, but there were times he would abstain as punishment. Now I realize that those were times when he had probably spent his lunch hour in his 'partner's' bed.

"After reading your comments in *Torn Asunder*, I am more convinced than ever that he has never understood the deep hurt he felt throughout his childhood. When I try to discuss it with him in my unprofessional way, he becomes very defensive, and the discussion ends with him still harboring all his wounds. This makes it easier for me to accept the emotional abuse he has showered on me, but it is not resolving his basic problem.

"Consequently, we feel that we need professional counseling more to help Reuben overcome the emotional trauma from his past and my trauma from the shock from which I have not been able to recover in the past year. Through God's mercy and grace our marriage is probably more intact than it ever was before. While I feel it is absolutely ridiculous that I let these actions so far in the past haunt me day and night, I cannot find release from it.

"I especially do not want our two children, four grandchildren, families or friends to know since they would be as devastated as I at the shock. As you can see, we need to discuss this with someone who has training and experience in dealing with long-term adultery and unresolved childhood emotional abuse."

NOTE

1. The National Center for Victims of Crime estimates that one in every three girls and one in every six boys are sexually abused before the age of eighteen; as cited in *Hush: Moving from Silence to Healing after Childhood Sexual Abuse*, Moody Publishers, © 2007 by Nicole Braddock Bromley.

DEVELOPMENT OF CLOSE CALLS

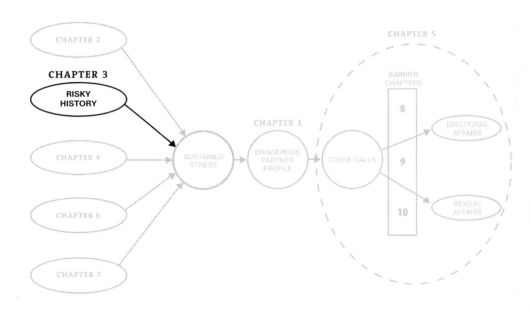

3 RISKY HISTORY:

Do You Have One?

We've talked about the risks of certain family history and also high-risk personal factors. But it isn't just the personal factors that can be risky. While a close call can often be the result of personal factors (and those are certainly a major part of the equation), there is usually a little more to it than that. Often there are situational factors that weigh heavily into the initiation of a close call. Let's move our discussion to two of these areas: high-risk times and high-risk behaviors.

HIGH-RISK TIMES

Times of Loss

If you recall what I said earlier—that sex is comforting, especially to males—then a season of significant loss is a high-risk time for close calls or even infidelity.

Unfortunately, this loss can affect both spouses to the degree that they cannot adequately care for or listen to or help the other in view of their own need. Each spouse can be too overwhelmed to even think of the other. Each is often just trying to survive and has very little left to give to their spouse.

Unfaithfulness or even flirtation, though certainly wrong, is understandable when you recall that sex is a great source of comfort. Research has identified that the frequency of sexual relations between husbands and wives tends to increase after the death of a significant family member. Though I am unaware of any research to substantiate the following claim, I suspect that this risk factor could be expanded to cover other severe reversals in areas such as health, occupation, finances, and social setting.

Life Transitions

Though life is basically one transition after another, I am talking about the big ones—retirement, major promotions, cross-country moves, caring for a chronically ill parent or child or even spouse, frightening lawsuits, and so forth. These kinds of experiences, both negative and positive ones, can have a significant impact on how we view ourselves and the level of support we have available. Some of these experiences can come with a sense of entitlement; with others, exhaustion; with others, the need to feel young and attractive. And any of them can make us vulnerable to another's attention. All of these transitions have a tendency to erode an individual's normal support systems.

Ron and Lori had lived all their lives in a midsized town in the northwest. They met in high school and both attended a local state university not far from home. The city's main employer hired Ron after graduation and, after a very successful career start, decided to transfer him to their corporate headquarters in a large city in the southeastern United States. Leaving the familiar family, church, schools, friends, and culture behind, they started a new life. Both felt they needed the change and both were quite excited about the opportunity. However, Lori decided to stay behind to finalize selling the house and finish the school year for the kids, so Ron went on ahead. In the months before Lori and the family joined him, he began to do things, go places, and engage in activities that he had to keep secret from his wife. The office atmosphere and values were nothing like his conservative, small workplace had been back home. When he was no longer able to keep the secrets, he confessed everything; and they both recognized that if they were going to save their marriage, they had to go back to what was familiar.

It doesn't have to be as extreme as Ron and Lori's story. It can be a simple dullness that sets into a marriage when the focus is upon rearing the children. When the couple makes the parenting project the primary task of their marriage, they have a tendency to ignore the spousal relationship. Then, as the children prepare to leave the home, there is a great risk for close calls, infidelity, or divorce. The parenting job is done, and there is very little reason for these two "strangers" to stay together.

Pregnancy

Though popular literature has often talked about midlife crises and the resulting close calls and infidelities, I have long suspected that there are other high stress seasons of life. One that has surfaced often in the counseling office, e-mail requests for help, and in presentations that I have made is the season of pregnancy. Some of you might be surprised, but it is not all that unusual as you think about it:

- The emotional focus of the wife changes at the confirmation of pregnancy. The husband is no longer the primary person in her life. She has a new baby coming.

55

- ▥ Her hormones began to change, and many wives report a lowered libido during pregnancy.

- ▥ Her shape also begins to change, and many husbands find their wives less visually appealing.

- ▥ Sometimes there is nausea, tiredness, and even required bed rest, all of which can make her less interested in being close to anyone.

- ▥ Various levels of discomfort usually occur in the latter stages of pregnancy.

- ▥ Then factor in the sleep deprivation, the different hormonal changes after delivery, the restrictions on sexual activity, the pressure of caring for a newborn, the excess weight of the pregnancy, and it is no wonder that the time during and after pregnancy can place very difficult stress on marital relationships. And many a mom of young children will tell you that her need to be touched is more than satisfied by having babies and toddlers crawling over her—something a husband doesn't always understand!

HIGH-RISK BEHAVIOR

We have looked at high-risk family of origin history, high-risk factors, high-risk times, and now we will take a look at high-risk personal behavior. This category is probably the most obvious to most people. But still, even here, it's worth seeing how behavior we may feel is harmless can easily lead to a close call—or worse.

Opposite-Sex Friendships

Though our culture talks a lot about platonic heterosexual friendships, I have become convinced that this is a dangerous experiment. One survey even shows that 50 percent of the pastors polled who acknowledged inappropriate sexual behavior while they were in ministry and married had a history of close female friendships. When you have a close opposite-sex friendship, you only manage one half of the experience. You have no control over what the other party brings to each engagement. It doesn't take much for the conversation to drift to personal issues, such as complaints about one's marriage. After all, that's what friends are for, right?

Workplace Affairs

About a third of men who admit to infidelity report they are dissatisfied in their marriage, while almost two-thirds of women report high levels of marital dissatisfaction prior to their affair.[1]

Don and Trish had remarried after many years of being single. Both of their initial spouses had left the marriages because of affairs. Both did a great job of raising their children as single parents, and now they were almost done. When they met at a trade show, there was an immediate connection due to having so much in common. After a whirlwind courtship and marriage, with the blessing of all their children, they settled back down into their respective careers. Now, after seven years, things were not going so well. Though no children were living in the home, many of Don's and Trish's differences were causing distance between the two of them. Trish felt too tired to be fun anymore. The new grandchildren, the adult children's schedules (six children between them!), and their own work schedules were taking their toll. On a business trip and after drinking too much at a dinner with clients, Don had a one-night stand with a coworker. Initially, he tried to pass it off as a common, sex-only affair in a sex-starved marriage, but, given both of their histories, Trish would not accept it. He had no interest in leaving the marriage; she had no interest in him staying.

Volunteer Opportunities

The Christian counterpart to the workplace affair occurs when two people have similar passions for volunteer service that they might not share with their individual spouses. The volunteer opportunity brings them together on a repeated basis, and they both begin to not only enjoy what they are doing but who they are doing it with. Over time, this mutual admiration, this shared passion and understanding, and the sense of achievement that comes with success, all coalesce into a relationship that invites inappropriate close calls.

It often starts innocently enough with the idea of planning how to do a better job in the volunteer opportunity. From there, it can quickly escalate to withholding conversational topics from the spouse in order to share them with the volunteer partner who "seems to understand me better." At this point an individual is robbing the marriage of the emotional intimacy it so desperately needs. When criticism of the marriage enters the conversation, even under the guise of "Help me understand my spouse better, will you?" then you are on a slippery slope to a full-blown affair.

"Soloing" in Public Places

One of the concepts that intrigued me early on in my counseling while listening to men and women who had been unfaithful in marriage was that very few of them were overtly looking for an illicit relationship. With my curiosity piqued, I listened with the purpose of trying to find out how these folks eventually "found" their affair partner. I found the answer to this question by asking an "other woman" who was sitting in my office.

She said, "It's easy. When I see someone sitting in a public place by themselves, I can immediately tell if they're happy or unhappy in their marriage."

Incredulous, I asked her, "You mean you can tell if someone's happy or unhappy in their marriage just by looking at them?"

She answered, "Yes, those people who are unhappy in their marriage send out signals that I pick up on!" She continued, "I would never strike up a friendship with someone I think might hurt me by rejecting my advances. I always make sure that they are dissatisfied at home early on in our conversations."

I did not believe this woman at first. But when I have shared this material with couples in which the adulterer was unhappy in the marriage, both of them agree strongly that this is exactly what happened. Over the years since that conversation, I have become convinced that this woman is right—people who are unhappy in their marriage send out signals of being in that frame of mind.

And there are people out there, in your world, who are looking for unhappy spouses. They will settle for someone they can make happy and someone who can make them happy for even a short period of time.

I have also come to believe the corollary to the above formula; namely, that those who are happy in their marriages have fewer temptations. The "other woman" or "other man" will not bother with them. It has very little to do with the attractiveness of an individual. It has everything to do with your mental state of mind about your marriage and the kind of signals you are sending to those in the world in which you live.

Newly married, and for the most part happy with his new bride, Trevor was still adjusting to his expectations of married life. For the past year and a half, he had eaten lunch out at the neighborhood diner close to work. He had become friends with all the waitresses, and they all knew the details of his impending marriage. Of course, when Trevor revisited the restaurant after the honeymoon, they wanted to know all about the marriage itself. He counted these gals his friends. Some of them were even old enough to be his mother, and he had known all of them longer than he had known Sara. He began sitting in the same section and continued to talk openly about his new marriage to one of the young waitresses who expressed a lot of interest. Today though, when she brought the check, she also dropped a hotel key beside his plate, said, "I'll see you at 3:00," and walked away!

Fantasizing

When you find your mind wandering into daydreams about someone who is not your spouse, you're in a dangerous spot. This can start innocently enough just by thinking about the other person: "I wonder what she's doing right now?" or "I hope I see him this morning at church." It can progress to comparisons that have you inserting this person in the place that should be reserved for your spouse: "If only my husband treated me the way Bobby treats Carla . . ." or "I wish my wife dressed more like Kathy—she understands how important appearance is to a man." From there it's not a big leap to move to daydreams or fantasies about a special friendship, connection, or even an intimate relationship.

Internet

In these days of Web mobility, you don't have to be in physical proximity to get involved with someone to the point of a close call. With chat rooms, finding an old classmate, and other avenues of communication, it's too easy to meet someone online who can draw you into a close call.

IDENTIFYING YOUR RISK

Let's put the information you learned in the last chapter together with what we've discussed in this chapter and see if and how you might be at risk for adultery. I know this sounds like a stark statement, but remember, my purpose here is to tell you what adulterers have been telling me for thirty years—there *are* risk factors that those who have affairs wish they had known so they could have been on guard against having a close call that led to the heartache of adultery. Not one person I've talked with and counseled did not have deep regret for the devastation caused by adultery.

Two clusters of these risk factors are part of your story: the personal history factors and the family history factors shown on the chart on pages 62 and 63. You can't change them, so just recognize, note, acknowledge, be aware of them, and move on.

However, you do have a lot of influence on the other two clusters: high-risk seasons and personal behavior items. The following chart is an opportunity for you and your spouse to privately identify what each of you think are the high-risk factors for yourself as well as for your spouse. Remember, it's not a matter of who is right or who is wrong. It's really a matter of understanding what each of you brings to the table, so read closely and learn. It's *what*, not *who*!

After identifying the risk factors for both you and your spouse, note your findings on the chart entitled "High-Risk Factors." Make notes and comments as they come to mind, and then the two of you need to sit down and talk about these issues. I remind you again that a risk factor does not determine that a close call or an affair inevitably lies in your future. In fact, the opposite is true if each of you will acknowledge what you bring to the marriage. Don't be defensive.

As the two of you talk about this, identify which item within each cluster is the primary risk to your relationship within that cluster. Give some thought as to why you've responded in the way you have, and listen to your mate's reasoning carefully.

Given their history, some people probably wonder how they managed to remain faithful in marriage as long as they have. It's worth keeping this in mind: the greater number of risk factors, without the same degree of awareness and protection, the

HIGH-RISK FACTOR

This checklist contains a cluster of experiences that help identify individuals at risk for infidelity. Simply mark each item YES or NO according to your personal history. In the right-hand column are brief definitions of the risk factors.

YES	NO	HIGH-RISK FAMILY HISTORY	DEFINITION/POTENTIAL RISK
☐	☐	Family history of infidelity	Up to two generations back
☐	☐	Single parent/blended family	A more vulnerable family history
☐	☐	Physically abusive/chronic conflict	Creates high need for nurturance and reassurance

YES	NO	HIGH-RISK PERSONAL FACTORS	
☐	☐	Sexual molestation	Childhood seduction, abuse, molestation
☐	☐	Adolescent promiscuity	Sexually active at fifteen or earlier, more than six partners in the teen years
☐	☐	Learning disabilities/ADHD	High need for reassurance and nurturance due to emotional pain

HIGH-RISK FACTORS (continued)

YES	NO	HIGH-RISK TIMES	DEFINITION/POTENTIAL RISK
☐	☐	Loss—death, health, occupational/career	Look to sex for healing and comforting
☐	☐	Life changes—pregnancy, school years, teens launching	Affair provides reassurance of youth, virility, attractiveness
☐	☐	Life transitions—moves, promotions	Loss of usual supports/controls

YES	NO	HIGH-RISK BEHAVIOR	
☐	☐	Opposite-sex friendship with private conversations	Always begins to mean more/comforting
☐	☐	Volunteer opportunity with opposite sex	A shared heart/passion that doesn't exist in the marriage
☐	☐	"Soloing" in public places	Needy individuals are more aggressive
☐	☐	Fantasizing about another	Erodes satisfaction with spouse

63

more likely an individual will have a close call with a dangerous partner. However, the more aware you are of your own risk factors, the more likely you'll be able to resist a close call situation or pull back from it if it occurs.

And don't discount the power of your moral compass or your religious convictions. Commitment to marriage has kept many husbands and wives faithful to each other despite family history, personal history, and high-risk seasons of life. However, research has shown — as have your own open eyes to the people around you — that close calls and adultery can sneak up almost before you're aware of what's happening. That's why it's essential to educate yourselves on these matters.

Now the next part can be tough stuff to talk about — sharing old history that most couples shove under the rug and never discuss. Many people don't talk about family history or personal history because they're not sure how their spouse will respond. If you will take time to talk through these things, though, you and your mate will know each other better, and you'll have an even stronger tie to the person with whom you've made a life-long commitment. In our culture these attractions occur regularly, and to discount or to deny their existence makes both spouses more vulnerable.

Deep inside of most of us is a yearning to be better known and still deeply loved for who we are; it is a place where no secrets are kept hidden and where your secrets have brought the two of you closer. Remember this as you talk over these things:

- How do you feel about the information you've uncovered in these last two chapters?
- Had you ever thought about these things contributing to your risk of looking outside your marriage to have any needs met, or even having an affair?
- Now that you're aware of your own risk factors, what are you going to do about it?

▨ What have you learned about your spouse that
   will help both of you be more protective of your
   relationship?

COULD THIS BE YOU?

"It happened two years ago when we lived on the East
Coast. I was in a really weird place in my life. My husband
and I had been trying at that point for a year and a half to
have a baby. I had weathered the sorrows of infertility fairly
well up until that point, but something happened. I believe I
slipped into a mode of bitterness and then soon into discon-
tentment. I wanted nothing more than to be where all my
friends were: home with their little ones. If I couldn't have
that, then I decided that I'd try to enjoy other realms of the
world. It is hard to describe or put into words, but I became
fascinated by earthly things. I started studying Jung and his
philosophies. I became really into recording my dreams and
trying to understand their meanings. I wanted to start traveling; I'd bug my husband about taking me to Italy or Spain
(knowing the timing wasn't right but not caring).

"I became completely wrapped up in one person—me. All
my pursuits were to make myself feel good. I soon started
feeling like my husband just couldn't understand me.

"During this time I met a much older man at work. He
had attended an Ivy League school, majored in philosophy,
and a was Buddhist. He was raised Christian but as an adult
he rejected it, so we would debate a lot. I'd tell myself that it
was good for me to talk to him about this because he might
come back to Christ. One day while on the phone with him, I
happened to stop for a light at the intersection where I attended church. I looked up, saw the church, and heard an au-
dible voice say to me, 'What are you doing?' It shocked me so
much that I asked him if he had heard anything. He said he

didn't, so I checked the radio, which wasn't even turned on. If I could go back in time I'd take a shovel and smack myself across the head. I won't go into details because frankly I don't want to relive it, but slowly, friendly debates at work became friendly debates at lunch or coffee. The final friendly debate was at his home where he physically came on to me. Soon, what I saw as fun became pretty scary, and I was in a situation that I didn't know how to get out of. I can honestly say I did not want anything to happen, and I fought him as well as I could, although some things did happen that make me really sad. I hate to think about that day. But I hate to think about the next day even more.

"The next day reality hit, and my world was shattered because for the first time in months, I saw clearly. Everything came crashing down. I reached out to my church and was able to meet right away with one of our pastors. She was such a minister to me. I told her everything; she prayed for me and in her wise counsel told me to tell my husband. That was the hardest thing I ever had to do. I don't like remembering that day because the pain still burns when I remember my husband's face. He was devastated. But because my husband is such a wonderful man, we were able to work through it and, to fast-forward for the sake of length, four months later I got pregnant. The joy God has given us in our son and our restored (and better) marriage is a testimony to His love and grace."

NOTE

1. *Infidelity: A Practitioner's Guide to Working with Couples in Crisis*, Paul R. Peluso, ed. (New York: Taylor & Frances Group, 2007), 3: "Men tend to engage in affairs in order to address sexual disappointment more than women do"; citing a study by Buunk and Dijkstra in 2004. About a third of men who admit to infidelity report they are

dissatisfied in their marriage, while almost two-thirds of women report high levels of marital dissatisfaction prior to their affair (Glass & Wright, 1992).

DEVELOPMENT OF CLOSE CALLS

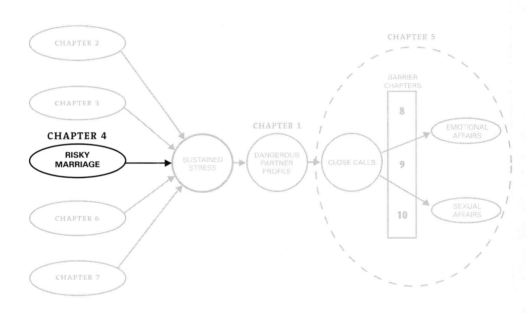

4 RISKY MARRIAGE:
Are You in One?

RANDY AND CINDY

It was a beautiful day in southern California, and Randy was enjoying his drive up the I-5. Putting the new Lexus on cruise control, he sat back and started reflecting on his life.

Three kids, all doing extremely well in school, heavily involved in extracurricular activities, looked up to as leaders in their local schools and headed for the best colleges. Cindy, well that's a bit of another story, he was thinking. She wasn't as happy as he would like to see her be, but then she's always been a bit of a worrier with a negative attitude. Pretty much the cup has always been half empty for her.

One thing, though, it had certainly been due to her extraordinary efforts that the kids were turning out so well. She certainly set him free to do whatever his career asked of him and, as a result, he'd risen to the top.

Yes, sir, he thought, twenty great years and counting.

Oh, there were some little things that he would like to see changed in the relationship, but overall he was very happy. He was grateful that his own family was so much better off than he had been growing up.

From Cindy's perspective, though, it was a different story. She didn't think she and Randy had much of a marriage at all, and she had decided early on that the problem wasn't just going to go away. She threw herself into the lives of her children, and since there was plenty of money, she soon learned to settle for the satisfaction that it could provide for her and the kids. Oh, she had asked that they seek counseling and had even suggested a couple of marriage-enrichment weekends, all to no avail. Randy just thought everything was fine and saw no need to have anybody else intrude into their great pattern.

But Cindy could see the good times quickly coming to an end. In five years the kids would be gone. She had started asking herself with increasing urgency, "Who am I and what am I going to do with all my time when the kids won't be here?"

Finding herself alone again—Randy was seldom able to join her—at one of her daughter's soccer games, she sat with another mom; their daughters were best friends. She started sharing some of the thoughts and feelings she was struggling with and, to her surprise, the other mom said she was in the very same boat.

A few weeks later, alone again at another soccer game, she saw the husband of the woman she had been talking with earlier. He waved, seemed so friendly, and came and sat down beside her. She had known both of them for years, and he opened the conversation with the comments that his wife had shared about their earlier conversation. He hoped she didn't mind, but he found it very interesting, so Cindy started sharing again. Suddenly, soccer games became a lot more appealing, and Cindy found herself looking forward to them more than ever. *Just a "male friend"* she thought. *Very safe.*

You can see it coming, can't you? It's a disaster in the making.

You probably found yourself saying, "No! No!" But why couldn't Cindy and Randy realize this? Why can't they understand, why aren't they aware of the distance and vulnerability they both have? Why are they so oblivious to the danger that lurks so close to their marriage?

Simply put, they've never taken the time to listen to the other's perception of their shared marital history. They have never been open to a review of their first twenty years. They decided to find satisfaction in their own private worlds.

A LOOK AT HISTORY

Let me assure you, you don't have to wait twenty years to benefit from a review of your history. In fact, you should do it at every major transition. A relationship needs lots of attention, or your perception of it will quickly become outdated and you will have no clue about what is really happening between the two of you.

You'll enjoy the following activity, which provides you with just such an opportunity. Look at the Marital Satisfaction chart. You will see a cluster of boxes across the bottom of the page and five horizontal lines across the top of the page with a 1 to 5 ranking.

You and your spouse will do the first part together, so get some refreshments and all the old picture albums or CDs. But first you will need to make one copy of this original for every five years that you have been married (if you lived together prior to marriage, you should count that time as part of what you're going to evaluate). So if you've been married twenty-five years, you'll need five of these sheets.

On each sheet, the dotted line boxes will represent the first six months of a given year, and the solid line box that follows is the last six months of that same year. Follow that vertical line to the top of the page and you will pass through a smaller box

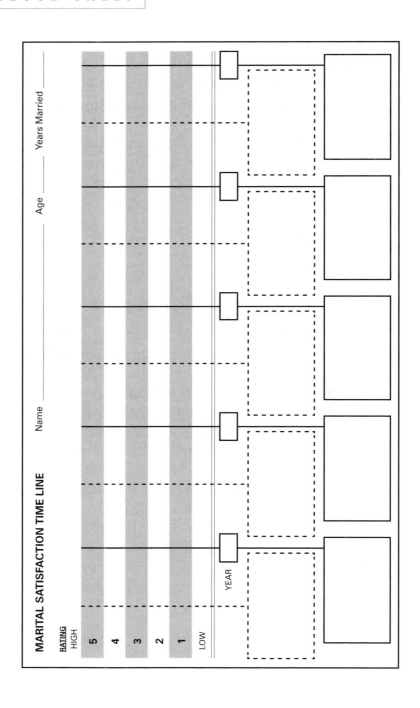

in which you can put the actual year, e.g., 1990. Now sit down together and fill in the boxes using the following list of topics placed at appropriate times in your history:

Post high school education
Births of children
Deaths of family members
Job promotions/losses/changes
Significant vacations
Moves
Major illnesses/accidents
Major financial or legal issues
Marital difficulties/counseling experiences
Living arrangements outside the nuclear family members
Other

Once the two of you have all the bottom boxes filled out to the best of your recollection, make a second photocopy of the entire set. Each of you, with your own set of charts and in private, then needs to put a dot on each vertical line (both dotted and solid lines) that best reflects your satisfaction with the marriage at the time of the events listed in the attached box.

Be honest. No matter what condition your relationship is in at this time, place yourself, to the best of your ability, back at the time period that you are marking on the chart. How did you feel at that time about the marriage?

When you have finished placing a dot on each vertical line, take a black pen and connect the dots. Tape the sheets together and presto! You have your individual Marital Satisfaction Time Line (MSTL).

To Think About

▨ What is your first impression as you look at your chart spread on the floor in front of you?

▧ How do you feel about sharing this with your spouse?

▧ Does any dot need to be adjusted to better reflect what you were experiencing at the time?

Many folks report surprise at seeing their own MSTL for the first time. It helps make sense of why they feel the way they do. It captures in black and white those often nebulous feelings that defy expression or rationale.

Overall Marital History

Before the two of you take a look at your joint marital history, it might be helpful to have an overview of how couples in general have reported marital satisfaction across their relationships.

American couples commonly report the highest level of marital satisfaction prior to children arriving in the home. Many marriages then report a gradual decline in marital satisfaction over time until the children begin to leave home following high school.

In our current culture this response might be changing because we are seeing young adults continuing to live with their families far beyond what was considered normal twenty years ago. However, assuming that children leave the home and do not return there to live, marriages at that time report a mixed response pattern. Some return to a high level of marital satisfaction very quickly, often within six months of the children's departure, while other marriages continue to deteriorate into dullness and even divorce.

Take the Plunge

Before the two of you dive into the discussion of your Marital Satisfaction Time Line chart, it is wise to remember the following points:

- It is normal for some decline in the marital satisfaction levels to occur across a couple's marital history.

- Remember that your initial perception upon viewing your spouse's pattern is probably not the same reaction you will have upon further reflection. This is a time to think about what you are seeing, to ask questions, to explore what was going on inside of your spouse, and not a time to draw conclusions. In other words, give your spouse the understanding that each of us so desperately wants. It is not a time to "try to get your point across."

- There are at least two, and probably more, different ways to view your marital satisfaction level at any given point in time. Remember, too, that even your families and friends have perceptions of your marital satisfaction level. So no single view of this level is the "right" one.

- The purpose of this exercise is not to argue for your view, but rather to discuss each other's perceptions of the relationship at various points in its history. This is a wonderful opportunity for the two of you and will help build your intimacy.

- I know this is hard to do, but don't take your spouse's comments personally. There are multiple reasons why each of you might have had the emotional response you experienced at a particular point in time. Don't try to argue your partner out of their viewpoint. Just listen and learn.

- On the other hand, don't criticize or blame your spouse for creating your dissatisfaction with the marriage during a particular experience. Again, there might have been multiple reasons why they could not have made it better for you at that particular point. Sometimes, we hit "the wall" and feel like all we can do is only take care of ourselves.

Choose a time to review the charts when you both are free from time constraints or pressure. Make sure that even after looking at the charts and listening to each other, you will still have time left to privately reflect on what you've seen and heard. Do not make any rash decisions. Most important, do not share this information with anyone unless you have your spouse's permission. To do that without permission is to erode the trust and confidentiality that should exist between a husband and wife.

Unwrap the Results

Okay, now it is time to take a look at your results together. Sitting on a couch, side by side, lay your MSTL on the floor in front of you.

- Try to capture your first impressions and share them with each other.
- Look for periods of high-level satisfaction (4 or 5) reported by both of you.
- Talk about your surprises. Ask questions about what your spouse was experiencing during those times.
- Notice the overall pattern. Is it one of similarity? Did the two of you experience the events in the boxes in a similar or dissimilar pattern? Why? Do you experience these normal ups and downs with the same level of intensity or is one spouse reporting significantly lower lows and higher highs than the other spouse? Why might that be true?
- Pay attention to the emotional tone of the relationship. What appears to bring the two of you the greatest

satisfaction and pleasure? Has your relationship followed a pattern similar to the one that most couples report? How do you feel about that? Have you both reported upswings in the emotional tone at various times in the marital history, or does the time line reflect a long and gradual deterioration?

- Take a look at the resiliency of your relationship. Has it ever hit bottom and recovered? Did you both experience the bottoming out at about the same level? Did you both recover to the previous high level of satisfaction? Did you recover at about the same pace? Talk about what you did to recover from the low point(s) in your history. If it was more significant for one spouse than the other, find out why.

Interpretation of Some Common Chart Lines

Remember Cindy and Randy at the beginning of the chapter? Their chart would probably look like this:

RANDY AND CINDY

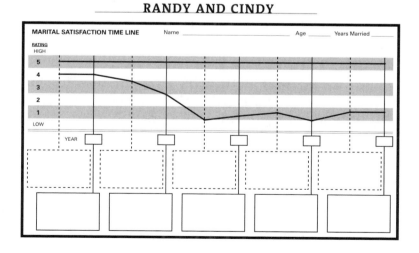

Randy was as happy as he could be. He would be shocked to realize how unhappy his wife really was with the marriage. When one spouse reports very high level satisfaction (5) and the other spouse doesn't reciprocate, it may indicate one or more of the following:

- I like the relationship just the way it is.
- I don't want to change it.
- It allows me to do what I have always wanted to do.
- The fact that we look good on the outside is all that matters.
- I am not responsible to contribute to the happiness in your life.
- Compared to my background, I'm as good as I can be.
- You are doing exactly what you are supposed to be doing; don't change.

It is this blindness and attitude set that allows adultery to flourish in what often looks like a great family. Two-thirds of your married life will be spent apart from raising children. Randy and Cindy have not addressed that reality.

You could say the same about Jack and Sue as well. Jack and Sue met when they were both home one summer from the different universities they were each attending. They hit it off immediately, and the summer turned out to be a great romance. It wasn't long, once they returned to their respective universities, that they decided to meet halfway for weekends together. Their sexual relationship created an artificial sense of closeness and, over time, prevented them from addressing the differences each brought to the relationship.

Even though they hadn't planned on getting married, when Sue became pregnant, they both decided that their romantic times together would form the basis of a good marriage. It wasn't long after the baby came, however, that they both realized this was going to be much more difficult than either had anticipated.

Sue dropped out of college, and Jack went to work part-time while he finished school. Sue got her mother to babysit so she could work as well. Too much responsibility, sleep deprivation, and disappointed dreams all combined to cause Jack and Sue to settle for less than either had wanted in a marriage.

Finally, some fifteen years later, Jack got involved with a coworker. Jack and Sue's MSTL looks like this:

JACK AND SUE

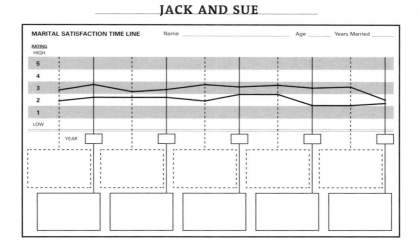

And this is what it says:

- I am worn out.
- I have nothing left to give.
- Don't expect anything from me.
- It is all I can do to make it through the day.
- Take care of your own needs.
- I am overwhelmed with my own responsibilities.
- You have given nothing to me and I have nothing to give to you.

- ▨ I will stay in this until the kids leave.
- ▨ One of these days, when I leave here/this marriage, I will be happy.
- ▨ This has never been good and I don't know how to change it.
- ▨ I forgot if we have ever been happy.
- ▨ I am not sure I ever loved you.

This is a marriage of obligation and commitment. There is something outside of this relationship holding it together (in this case, the children). There is no fun and pleasure in the spousal relationship.

Many times these spouses carry on like good roommates or neighbors, efficient and effective, but without any feeling for each other. Sometimes their commitment to each other is sufficient to keep them from adultery, for a while. Invariably, though, they begin to say to themselves, "I don't want to be in a stagnant relationship like this for another fifteen years."

When husbands or wives get involved in this type of self-talk, they are extremely susceptible to close calls.

Tim and Amanda thought they had done everything right. They were still virgins when they married, they went through premarital counseling, they waited to get married until they were through college, and they both had good jobs when they said their vows.

However, it wasn't long until difficulties with their extended families began to affect their relationship. Amanda's parents divorced. Mom, with no career skills and a daughter in high school, moved in with them. The condo was very crowded, but both agreed that it was the right thing to do.

Shortly after that, Tim's twin brother went through a separation, and they found themselves spending many hours supporting him, inviting him over for dinner, and in general trying to encourage him. Amanda's younger sister, meanwhile, was having a difficult time emotionally trying to live back and forth between her mother and father—two different homes with two very different sets of rules.

Tim was helpless trying to enforce the guidelines he and Amanda thought important. And Amanda didn't feel like she wanted to be her sister's mother while their mom was away at work in the evenings. In the first few years of this marriage, it is easy to see how Tim and Amanda had very little time to themselves in which to build a good history.

When Amanda got pregnant with their first child, Tim felt even more responsibility to provide for his extended family. Working harder, taking overtime, it was not long before he felt like giving up. Amanda was sick a lot in the pregnancy, and, though he knew it wasn't her fault, he began to feel like they had little in common anymore.

At home one night and on the computer, he decided to look up some old college friends from happier times. It didn't take long to locate old classmates, girls and guys, some who even lived in the neighborhood. After a few short weeks of e-mailing one in

TIM AND AMANDA

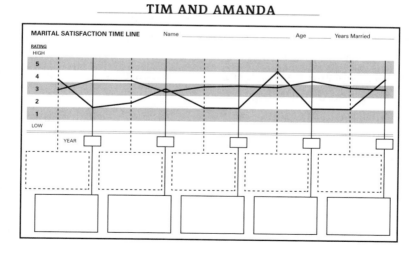

particular, he decided to drive by her house. Within a few weeks this close call turned into an affair. This is what their MSTL looked like.

Here is what it says:

- We can't say no to outside intrusions.
- We feel responsible for everybody else but ourselves.
- This too will pass, but we will be too tired to care.
- How did we get into this mess anyway?
- You helped with my family; I guess I have to help with yours.
- This is not worth it.
- Where were you when I needed you most?
- You are staying at work in order to stay away from home.

PUTTING AFFAIR COMPONENTS BACK INTO YOUR MARRIAGE

One of the reassurances that couples sometimes forget to practice, especially during times of increased stress, is to take time alone doing what they like doing best. In fact, most of these high-level periods of mutual satisfaction naturally include the precise elements found in affairs. You can think of these affair-type components as childhood magic, adolescent sexuality, and adult mobility.

Childhood magic is freedom from responsibility and the schedules that so easily consume you at home. It encourages the two of you to come and go when you want, to eat and drink what you like, to get up when you want, to stay up all night if you wish, and to simply indulge yourselves in "whatever your little hearts desire." God knows His children need relaxation and fun. There are even some pretty great examples of this in the Bible. In fact,

He prescribed many of Israel's festivals for just that purpose.

You've probably seen couples on airplanes and in restaurants, acting as though they were in their "own little bubble," oblivious to all of those around them. You need this kind of childhood magic periodically in your relationship. You had it when you dated. It will energize you, build great memories for the two of you, and create anticipation for the next time you experience it.

Adolescent sexuality is chaotic, unplanned, spontaneous, and oblivious to the circumstances. It is lustful, passionate, and totally caught up in the moment. Can you imagine you and your spouse spicing up your sex life like this? Some surveys indicate that better than 90 percent of the couples involved in an affair report having sexual activity in their cars. When was the last time you, as a married couple, did that, or made love in

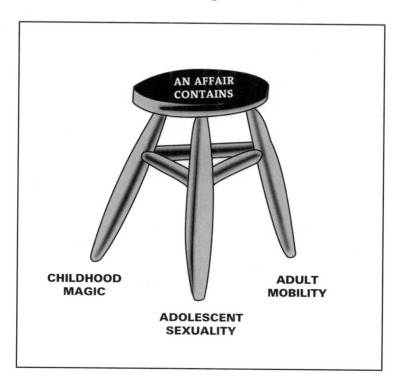

AN AFFAIR CONTAINS

CHILDHOOD MAGIC

ADULT MOBILITY

ADOLESCENT SEXUALITY

some other unconventional place? Sex that routinely occurs between the sheets, in the dark, behind locked doors, and after the kids are asleep can become very boring.

Adult mobility is that final leg of this three-legged stool. It is that component of traveling together, of meeting at a hotel in your same town just to be with each other for a few hours, of taking a weekend break at a classy B&B, or of even just sneaking home during the day while your kids are still in school. It is going with your spouse on a business trip, even if he or she is tied up during most of the day.

If you were having an affair and had an hour and a half for lunch, and it took you a half hour to drive each way to see your partner, you would make the drive just to be with each other for the remaining half hour. When was the last time you made that kind of effort to see your spouse? Surprise each other. See each other outside the normal times you meet. It is exactly what you might do to see your partner if you were in an affair, so create some fun and the unexpected with your mate!

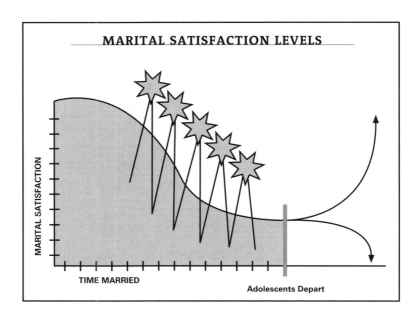

Those little "bursts" at the top of each spike contain the three components I just mentioned: childhood magic, adolescent sexuality, and adult mobility. Make your satisfaction chart look like this. Spend money on your marriage. Organize times like this with each other on a regular basis. Don't wait for a future season if you're going through a stressful period. Do something now. Do what it takes to nurture both of you and the relationship. It will drain the intrigue from the dangerous partner's profile.

 **IN SUMMARY**

Well, what does your chart say to the two of you? Are you happy with the message? Have you grown stronger and closer after difficult times? Do you need to do some things differently? What are you doing in preparation for that time period when the kids are gone?

All marriages go through good and bad seasons. But knowing this doesn't mean that most relationships are prepared for the tough transitions. Preparation only happens on purpose. Just like retirement planning, a little bit of investment over a long period of time pays great dividends. Grow your history of couple closeness. Create those spikes of high-level marital satisfaction. Spend money on your marriage.

COULD THIS BE YOU?

Though both in their late sixties, Danny and Janice highlight for us that close calls are often just over the horizon. As a little boy, Danny had learned to comfort himself when punished by looking at catalogs of women's underwear. Locked in his parents' bedroom, he began to create a long history of fantasy that eventually led him to an adulterous situation. His wife, Janice, though aware of the affair, stayed married to Danny and attempted to make the relationship good. She raised four children, worked full-time at a stressful job, developed lupus, but finally was able to retire. Meanwhile, some of their old friends who lived across the country called and asked if they could visit. The wife of this couple had cancer, and she wanted to travel while she was able.

This is where we'll pick up the story told in Janice's own words. As you read, notice the stressors, the simple way that fun can turn bad, and the fact that commitments to stay pure often don't stand up when in the presence of the dangerous partner.

Janice says,

"When our friends returned home, he and I began to e-mail each other. At first it was just friendly chatter, but soon it became more than that. Within a short time, we were spending large blocks of time talking on the phone and e-mailing each other several times a day. Even though he was a thousand miles away, we developed an emotional affair. After several months I went to the Midwest to attend my class reunion, which was in a nearby town. While there I visited him and intended to keep our relationship pure. Sadly, that was not the case. Between my own dissatisfaction with my marriage and my friend's wife's unavailability to him due to her illness, we were both vulnerable.

"Our e-mail relationship went on for another year before my husband found out about it.

"I found it very difficult to think that I had to come back to this marriage after all that had transpired. I had spent a considerable amount of time comparing my husband to my friend. I was upset by the fact that Danny had never gotten a 'real' job that brought in a steady, dependable paycheck. My friend, in contrast, had always had steady jobs and faithfully supported his family, sometimes with great sacrifice.

"The comparisons went on. I found love that I had not felt

in our marriage for many years. Why should I throw that away? I had compartmentalized my life in such a manner that I could be married to Danny and still carry on my relationship with another man.

"At this point I knew I must end the affair, but how could I? This was a very kind, loving man, who had never spoken to me with an anger or rage such as Danny had expressed. I was deserting the man who seemed to love me the most. I was so confused! How was I going to do this? I told my friend that it had to end, but my heart was still conflicted. It was the most difficult thing I had ever done, but with God's help, I was able to seek forgiveness from his wife and end that relationship. I was beginning to see that God had changed Danny's heart and life, and that he was, once again, becoming the man he was when I married him.

"There are two things about my experience I have come to realize. First, if this can happen to me, this can happen to anybody. I was raised in a Christian home and attended church ever since I was six years old. Having an affair with another man was not something that a Christian should ever do, and certainly, I never thought I would do such a thing. Second, many such affairs start very innocently, as mine did. Before I hardly knew what was happening, I was in over my head and was about to drown. My illicit relationship seemed thrilling and exciting at the time, but in the end, it brought great sorrow and destruction to our marriage. I can't tell you how glad I am that we survived."

SECTION 2:
Close Call Chemistry

DEVELOPMENT OF CLOSE CALLS

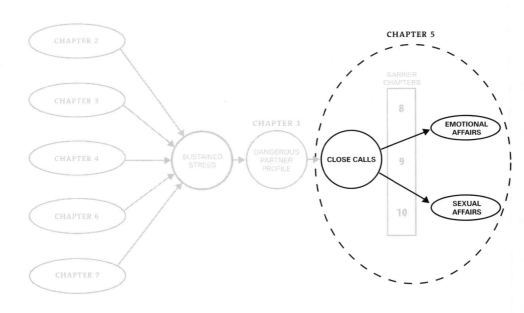

5 CLOSE CALLS and the Affairs They Can Lead To

We've heard about Carmen, Sam, Jody and Steve, Trent and Sally, Tim, and others. Some went through close calls and stopped there. Others took what could have been a close call and progressed downward into adultery.

So what exactly is a close call? Is it the same for everyone? Do all close calls go through a similar development?

CLOSE CALL CHARACTERISTICS

Yes, close calls are virtually all alike. They begin with an attraction to somebody other than your spouse that causes you to think about your time with this individual simply for the pleasure that it provides you. Maybe you're having regular meetings with someone of the opposite sex for business, shared interests, or volunteer opportunities.

In other words, you start to daydream about this person. It is not just the thought "Boy, is he good looking" or "Wow, she's gorgeous," but rather it is the reflection on the individual that results from the initial contact.

Somewhere in this phase, a friendship ceases and a close call starts. Now you're saving topics of conversation for this person. Your conversations progress from merely topics related to your mutual interest to far-ranging ones — and soon into personal issues. The reflection on personal life will cultivate the relationship. You scheme and plan on how to be together more often, for more time, without raising anyone's suspicions. There may be rituals unique to this relationship:

> "Hank and I meet at the break room for coffee at nine every Monday morning and talk about our weekend. If I get there first, I pour him coffee in that mug he likes. I make sure to keep plenty of hazelnut cream in the fridge since that's his favorite."

> "Judy and I always have a lot of business matters to talk about, so we started having lunch at the restaurant across the street so there are no distractions. I call her cell to let her know when I'm ready to leave; that way, we can just slip out without anyone interrupting."

These types of relationships easily become close calls. As time goes on, there is mutual admiration and a growing number of shared secrets.

At this point, many folks go into denial about how much the relationship is beginning to mean to them and only upon the final phase, evaluation, does a person often recognize how close he or she really came to adultery.

TRACKING THE PHASES OF A CLOSE CALL OR AN AFFAIR

Hank's and Judy's friends above may not have realized the extent of their feelings for the other person. It was just friendship, or just a business relationship. But if left to progress, these relationships could easily have gone from friendship to a natural progression to the point that both parties will share their mutual feelings of attraction for each other—the start of an emotional affair.

Let's look now at the four different phases of this dangerous sequence:

1. Growing mutual attraction
2. Entanglement
3. Destabilization of the relationship
4. Termination and resolution

Phase 1: Growing Mutual Attraction

Many times when men and women who have had affairs are telling their story, they begin by saying, "It all started so innocently. . . ."

After all, most people who commit adultery are not out looking to do so. But because we all are sexual creatures, created by God with that dimension of our personality, some sexual attraction toward another person (even though we are not married to that person) is natural. Those who cannot accept that such feelings are normal will often deny their existence. Christians especially hate to acknowledge this sexual attraction. Denial becomes the defense mechanism of choice.

Yet denial doesn't solve anything. Just because you don't acknowledge, even to yourself, that you feel the attraction doesn't mean that the attraction has stopped developing. In fact, it usually intensifies the problem. When you're in denial, the desire to be around the other person "goes underground," and contact with that person is often initiated unconsciously.

Phase 2: Entanglement

This is the infatuation phase. It begins with verbal signals. That's a good reminder for married couples!

Fantasy creeps in here very quickly too. Eventually, Phase 1 — Growing Mutual Attraction — moves to Phase 2 — Entanglement — when the future adulterer shares these feelings of attraction with their potential partner. Those feelings might be couched in an intended compliment such as, "If I wasn't married, I would think of marrying you," but nevertheless the message to the dangerous partner is that you *are* thinking about him or her.

Those who have slipped from a close call into a full-blown adulterous affair have told me that this is the point, mutual acknowledgment, at which everything changes: the e-mails, the voice mails, the verbal comments, the meetings, the lunches; all become saturated and supercharged with emotion. They mean way too much, much more than they should. Still, the denial of it all allows the emotional intensity to grow to the point that it appears that a "spontaneous combustion" occurs the first time they become sensual with each other. The denial is so powerful that if you told this adulterer-to-be that within twenty-four hours he would violate his own values, threaten his marriage, and risk his career, he or she would deny it.

Phase 3: Destabilization of the Relationship

Most affairs, even one-night stands, have "on-again, off-again" periods when the partners withdraw from each other and try to stop the relationship, even on the single night they might be together. When continued over long periods of time, these emotional attachments can become so intense and consuming that physical health suffers, emotional well-being and job production decline, these people can no longer think rationally, and they destroy other lifelong friendships.

Being with this other person seems to bring healing to life's hurts, as well as comfort and security. This other person causes them to feel cared for and cuts them loose from all the world's responsibilities. The two of them have created their own little world. This is what we all yearn for in our marriages—the "I need you" feeling, not the "I'm too busy; I don't care what you do" response. It is the desire to be wanted!

In healthy marriages, there is a balance between these feelings and the compulsivity that is so apparent in an affair. But on the other hand, the one thing I find so intriguing when I talk with adulterers is what they all seem to have in common: the passion they have for their partners. I cannot tell you how many times I've thought to myself when listening to their stories, *If I could just figure out a way to help couples develop these same feelings for each other on some kind of a regular basis, then all the need for marital counselors would disappear!*

Actually, the destabilization process reflects what can happen in a good marriage. In their effort to return to normalcy, most affair partners in this stage try to refocus on the demands of life. But due to all the mixed feelings in the relationship (fear, guilt, infatuation, shame, anger, exhaustion, and so on), they cling to each other in unhealthy ways for reassurance. However, if a marriage can take the good from this process—the periodic intense passion and love for each other—and leave all the desperation and negative feelings out of the picture, the married couple will be on their way to building a great relationship.

Phase 4: Termination and Resolution

A good marriage doesn't have to go through this phase. Most affairs do. Even those couples whose affairs resulted in marriage have a difficult time building and maintaining the trust, respect, and safety that the affair initially appeared to provide.

Without commitment, sexual passion creates an artificial sense of closeness. It is the sexual tension in a dating relationship that provides the energy for the couple to work through the differences in their backgrounds, their goals and values, and so forth — this is how couples build a solid foundation. Too often, though, these same couples, after marriage, don't continue creating the passion that an affair provides. They had it once and they let it die.

I think this is why most adulterers coming back to their marriage work so hard at rebuilding what they once had. It might sound very strange to you, but in most cases the passion of the affair was what was missing in the marriage.

FOUR CLASSES OF AFFAIRS

You'll find it interesting to learn that there are four types of extramarital affairs. Counselors find that these descriptions help them portray for their clients more clearly how an affair developed and ended.

Having knowledge about these will help you see just where there might be risk for falling into an affair, and you'll see spelled out what components are involved in each type. The stories that illustrate each affair will show you how real people can so easily get swept up to the point of adultery.

CLASS 1: One-Night Stand

This type of affair is obviously unplanned. It often involves partners who didn't even know each other prior to the affair. It is done in utmost secrecy, and it's not an overstatement to say that this type of affair often, though not always, results from alcohol consumption. This type of affair contains no emotional involvement, is self-serving, and does not come with a desire to perpetuate closeness. This type of affair has all the components of a "first love" type of sexual experience. Our sexually saturated culture feeds especially into this type of affair, and it is the one-night stand that usually results in immediate and intense remorse. Bill's story illustrates how quickly a one-night stand type of affair crept up on him.

Exhausted, Bill decided to return to his hotel for a brief nap prior to grabbing a bite to eat in preparation for the evening's seminar. Upon arriving in his room, he noticed the red message light flashing; his wife had been trying to reach him throughout the afternoon.

When he called her back, he realized from her tone of voice that Gwen was both angry and hurt that he had to be gone from home again. As he hung up the phone in discouragement, Bill reflected on how exciting it had been when he had taken this new job several years ago. The pay increase was phenomenal, the relocation in new quarters sounded attractive; but the side effects—the family concerns, mainly—had been pretty negative.

He tried to fall asleep, but now his mind was racing and he couldn't. Finally, in frustration, he jumped off the bed and decided to go eat a little early—maybe that would make him feel better. Due to the early hour, the restaurant was nearly empty. Maybe here in this peaceful spot he could find some rest from all the turmoil he was feeling inside.

Why did Gwen have to call and dump all that stuff on me anyway? He felt bad that she had to be home alone, but he also felt angry because they had decided to take the new career position together, both of them knowing a lot of travel would be involved. Why couldn't she live up to her part of the bargain?

He felt torn. And the more he thought about it, the more stirred up he got inside. Scanning the menu didn't help either. What normally would have been a fun part of his day—enjoying some good food—had suddenly turned flat.

Only after the waiter departed did Bill notice the attractive woman sitting across the aisle and down one booth. She was busy making notations on some reports. Unaware of his glance, she remained engrossed in her work.

Wow, she looked so in control of what she was doing, so professional and, Bill had to admit, quite attractive. He couldn't help but notice that she wasn't wearing a wedding ring. She was quite a bit younger than he was. Somebody's going to be lucky to have her as a wife someday, he thought.

His mind drifted back to Gwen and how she used to appear so efficient and attractive when they first met. But family wear and tear had taken its toll. Then again, he mused, he wasn't all he used to be either. He cast another glance at the woman and, as if by some magic cue, she looked up at the same time. The meeting of their eyes frightened him, and he immediately looked away.

In the moments that followed, Bill couldn't believe the sudden rush of emotion he felt. He hadn't felt so anxious since he was in high school. He didn't even know this woman; he'd only seen her five minutes ago. Irrationally, he felt sure that she could see his heart pounding wildly in his chest.

Get a grip. Stop acting so foolish and juvenile. He tried to change the focus of his thoughts. He had no luck. Over his coffee cup, he found himself glancing at her again. From then on, it was just a matter of time before their eyes connected.

She smiled, and he reciprocated. She started some innocent small talk across the empty aisle; they were both on business trips, both in sales. Innocently, she asked whether he cared to join her at her table. Why not? It was nice to meet a fellow business traveler in a near-empty restaurant. Amazingly, Bill found himself thoroughly enjoying the stranger's company. She often traveled on business and was married too. They had a little wine and a few laughs with their supper. Like cool water on parched ground, Bill soaked up her company and felt thoroughly refreshed by the time the checks came.

When she invited him to her room for an after-dinner drink,

he knew he shouldn't go, that in fact he had probably gone too far already. For a brief instant he teetered on the knife's edge of the decision. But in his confused mind he didn't much care anymore about keeping the rules. *I haven't felt this alive and vibrant in years. I'll accept her offer, just this once. I'll miss the seminar, but I can always order the tape. This won't get out of hand.*

But it did get out of hand. A few hours later, all those alive and vibrant feelings were gone. He had lost all control in the intoxication of the moment. As he rushed to dress and depart later that evening, she was hurt that he was leaving so quickly and not spending the night; he was angry at her and furious at himself. He felt so full of turmoil that he thought he would explode. How he hated himself for what he had done.

CLASS 2: Entangled Affair

This type of affair develops gradually. The emotional involvement is intense; perhaps there are family of origin deficits that contribute to the emotional need that has been fed by this more complex relationship. Such an affair might last for a year or even two. Sexual activity is not immediate, as in a one-night stand, but occurs only later in the relationship, after a friendship is clearly established. The story of Rob and Becky and Becky's boss, George, illustrates this type of affair.

Rob was in graduate school at night and working full-time. Becky was doing quite well in her career and had enough going on that she was able to hide her disappointment in Rob's over-involvement in his work and studies. They had talked about this season in their lives beforehand, and both knew that it was going to be tough.

But somehow Becky just couldn't help feeling utterly unimportant to her mate and left out of Rob's daily life. She told herself, *Once school is over it'll get better. Better to go along now than to rock the boat. Rob has enough to worry about without a whining wife added.* So she tried to hang on and wait for the situation to improve.

Instead, it got worse. When graduate school was over, Rob began to study intensively for state certification. Licensing would take another two years of internship. When that began to sink in, Becky started to feel as if she were at the end of her rope. *Another two years? I don't know if I can last that long; I'm dying on the vine.*

She tried to discuss her feelings of desperation, isolation, and emotional fatigue with Rob, but there was so little time. So she shared her frustration and disappointment with her girlfriends at work. If Rob wouldn't listen, at least they would.

Apparently one of them mentioned it to George, her boss. George called Becky into his office one afternoon and gently probed about how she and Rob were doing. Becky didn't intend to, but right then and there she broke down and wept. George seemed so kind and understanding. He even offered to take her out to supper that night while Rob was at school. Tearfully, she accepted.

Soon their suppers together became a regular feature in Becky's needy life. Their times together made work more pleasant, and it gave her something to look forward to, instead of the lonely evenings to which she was accustomed. Rob never got home earlier than 10:00 p.m. and was usually so exhausted that he really didn't seem interested in hearing about her day anyway.

As Becky and her boss got to know each other better, they began to really hit it off. Before long, they started exchanging little hugs upon separating after dinner. Though she felt guilty about it, Becky found herself thinking about him more and more. She valued their newly escalated relationship a lot — maybe too much. But she tried to put her worries out of her mind.

George apparently felt the same way she did. One night at dinner, he revealed his feelings for her, and she had to admit that she felt the same for him. That evening when they left the restaurant, they decided to go to his apartment, and there they lost all control. Becky hurried home late at night and felt lucky to arrive before Rob did.

After that, she abandoned her restraint. Her life became centered around George and the time she could spend with him. For the first time in years, she felt alive and in love. She was beside herself with infatuation and found herself thinking constantly of ways to make their relationship more fun and exciting. She bought new clothes, began to get back in shape, and started having her hair done regularly the way George liked it.

Rob liked the "new" Becky as well, but he interpreted the new behaviors as Becky finally coming to grips with his schedule and internship. He felt now that he could begin to concentrate on his studies without worrying about how Becky was feeling. This continued for months until the second time that Becky almost didn't make it home to their apartment before Rob did.

Becky knew she had to quit seeing George outside the office, so they decided to call it off. They both felt guilty enough to agree readily to such a plan.

But it didn't last long. Two days later, George called her into his office to say he just couldn't end it that quickly. Through all those great dinner conversations, her friendship had become very meaningful to him. "Couldn't we just be friends?" he suggested. "We can talk during dinner and then just say good night."

Becky wanted to maintain their relationship just as badly as he did. So, mustering all her willpower, she agreed to try it. But that night they ended up at his apartment once more. Again she was able to beat Rob home. But the next morning at the office, George called her and apologized for not holding up his end of the bargain and suggested that maybe they needed a break from each other for a week or two.

By this time Becky was thoroughly confused. Her feelings

for George were becoming stronger every day. She reluctantly agreed to the "trial separation," even though the previous night with him was so perfect that she had entertained the idea that George was "the one" for her.

A week went by, and Becky found herself desperate just to talk to him. Finally, she couldn't stand it anymore. She called him on the intercom, and when he answered, she couldn't believe the rush of feeling she experienced upon simply hearing his voice.

During their conversation in his office, she could hardly control herself. Reflecting later, she was shocked at her lack of self-control and stewed about it all night, losing precious sleep. *Why am I so obsessed about our relationship?*

By the next morning—dragging herself to work after a sleepless night—she knew she had to end it.

After work that day, she called and said good-bye. George argued that his feelings were involved and that it wasn't fair to end it so quickly. But Becky just hung up. She knew it wouldn't work; they had tried self-control, and it never worked.

Then, rather suddenly, George was promoted to a new division and transferred to a new office across the country. She just had to call and offer congratulations. His immediate response was "come with me." Overwhelmed and feeling more confused than ever, she said she would have to think about it. When she got home that night she told Rob she needed "some space." She had to get away and think about what she really wanted for her life. She felt sorry to see the hurt look in Rob's eyes, but she also knew there was very little left of the relationship they once had.

CLASS 3: Sexual Addiction

An affair under this class often starts in childhood or early adolescence with inappropriate sexual exposure. It eventually develops a ritualistic pattern of acting out. It is a sex-only experience and is never satisfying. It is not about emotional attachment and is self-serving. It is always about the addict and never about the spouse. This type of affair is another outcome of our sex-obsessed culture.

This behavior is an attempt to self-medicate shame, anxiety, and depression. When women experience these feelings, they tend to eat. When men do so, they act out sexually. Sex is the best antidepressant medication known to males, at least initially. Being freed from sexual addiction usually requires professional therapy to sort through all the contributors to it, then a maintenance group such as a twelve-step model.

A typical scenario of sexual addiction might play out this way....

Though excited about being married, Todd quickly realized that his mother-in-law meant as much or more to his wife than he did. His in-laws visited every weekend, and all the holidays required a barbecue at Mom and Dad's house. It was as though Sherry, his wife, had never left home. Todd was a quiet guy, though, and kept his feelings to himself. In fact, he had always prided himself on being unemotional. His job required that, and he was a very good at keeping his feelings out of the circumstances that needed his attention.

When Todd's company was bought out, he was let go. He found other work right away, but by that time Sherry's mother's health was failing and required a lot of her attention.

It wasn't long until Todd found himself visiting an old haunt from college days—the local massage parlor. He always hated the guilty feelings he had later. He knew Sherry would be disappointed if she found out, and he often promised himself that he would not go again. But he did. Every time things became difficult, he found himself visiting the place weekly for months on end before he stopped.

Sherry was busy with the three children, homeschooling, her mother's declining health, and a part-time job that she held on the weekends. She loved her life and assumed Todd loved his as well. Todd made a very good living for them all and appeared to enjoy his work even though it required very long hours. There were times that Sherry felt some misgivings about the growing distance between them, but she always managed to brush it off with the thought that this was just a season of life for the two of them.

Todd had never had many male friends, and he had very little interest in most sports. As a tech guy, he liked reading scientific and engineering magazines but was conversant in other subjects as well.

As the children got older and Sherry became increasingly distant, Todd found himself visiting the massage parlor more frequently. It was where he could reassure himself that he was an okay guy, where what he wanted mattered, where somebody cared for him, where he could get rid of those lonely feelings, and where he was known on a first-name basis. It became his haven away from work prior to going home.

Initially it was the bright light in his day, something he eagerly anticipated starting each morning. It was becoming more frequent, though, and it was starting to cost a lot of money. The girls did not seem as nice to him as they used to be. Often, he would leave feeling taken for granted and disappointed with the experience. "Maybe I need to find a new place. Maybe I need to try some different things." He had always promised himself that he would never mix pornography with his business and uncertain where to go or what to do, he returned time after time to this disappointing experience. Finally, he gave in and started using the Internet. Initially, he had a satisfying response, but before long he was spiraling out of control.

CLASS 4: Add-on Affair

This affair occurs to satisfy a specific void. It develops when a spouse shares an emotionally satisfying experience with an acquaintance because the other spouse has no interest in participating in this activity. This experience is initially platonic, such as a hiking club, a worship team, a shared ministry, a common leisure pursuit, and so on. Because participants in this kind of affair generally do not meet outside of the experience they find so satisfying, they consider the other a friend rather than a lover. They have no intention of leaving their spouses and family, and often feel they have done nothing wrong. Also, the sexual activity is often infrequent and dissatisfying to one partner, and is often provided out of obligation or for the purpose of maintaining the friendship. Invariably, however, in addition to the adultery, these relationships rob the marriage of emotional content. Jenna and Larry's story is an example of this type of affair.

John and Jenna had the ideal marriage. All of their children were adorable. Dad coached all the kids' athletic teams, and Mom with the golden voice was an enthusiastic participant on the church's worship team. A lot of men were intimidated by singing with Jenna—then Larry came along. Finally, she found a voice that matched her own, and the two of them sang beautifully together. The music director was thrilled. The congregation was transported upward. The more they sang, the more people asked for them to perform. Folks began to expect perfection, and rehearsals were becoming longer and more frequent.

One evening rehearsal was just not turning out right. Still working on it, they soon found themselves alone in the music room. Finally, Larry laughed and said, "Let's quit and sing something we know well so that we can go home happy."

That started a tradition. Every rehearsal now ended with fifteen or twenty minutes of singing together for fun. Sometimes a few of the team members would stay and listen, but on other occasions it was just the two of them. Those times started meaning a lot, and both Larry and Jenna wondered if the other felt it as strongly as they did. They would squeeze each other's hand as they left, but nothing beyond that.

Occasionally, the various worship teams would have social outings that spouses would attend. Jenna's husband, John, and

Kaye, Larry's wife, would often joke about the need for the two of them to find something to do together while Larry and Jenna were rehearsing. But everything was open and aboveboard, and respectful friendships developed between John and Larry and the wives, Jenna and Kaye.

One evening, after their fun sing, Larry asked Jenna if she would like to go out for coffee. He said Kaye was out of town with the kids, and he would enjoy her company prior to going home to an empty house. After calling John, who was watching a playoff game on TV, Jenna accepted. Thus began a sporadic but endearing set of conversations that ranged far beyond their shared love for music.

Eventually, over time, these conversations drifted into the topic of each other's marriages. They came to know each other too well. They began to save conversational topics for just these after-rehearsal coffees. They developed an intense friendship. They slipped into an emotional attachment that Larry especially was finding difficult to not sexualize.

They both reassured each other that they were still crazy in love with their spouses. They never talked about marriage to each other, and they were very cautious not to touch each other. But over time even that boundary was eroded. They felt so close to each other that their touching gestures became those of very close friends.

This "close call" relationship started stepping over the sexual boundaries two or three times a year at choir retreats, music conferences, and concerts. Though both would be hurt afterward, their friendship would bring them back together. This extramarital relationship contaminated almost fifteen years of their marriages to their spouses, and when exposed, it generated an emotional disaster in their community.

FOUR TYPES OF EXTRAMARITAL AFFAIRS

	CLASS 1 ONE-NIGHT STAND	CLASS 2 ENTANGLED AFFAIR	CLASS 3 SEXUAL ADDICTION	CLASS 4 ADD-ON AFFAIR
DESCRIPTION	One-night stand	Addictive relationship	Multiple partners	Satisfies a specific void
DEVELOPMENT	Immediate	Gradual	Impulsive	Gradual, focus on marital void
EMOTIONAL INVOLVEMENT	None	Intense	None	Intense, with narrow boundaries
SEXUAL ACTIVITY	Single experience; intense, lustful, passionate	Only much later in relationship; after friendship established	Immediate with multiple partners and increasingly distorted sexual activity	Irregular, often without mutual enjoyment
FAMILY OF ORIGIN DEFICIT	None	Emotional deficits create vulnerability	Sometimes an influence	Emotional deficits create vulnerability
REMORSE/ REPENTANCE	Usually immediate and intense	Initially none; initial grief is for lost relationship; later grief is possible	Only after acting out internal tension builds to another episode	Regular, but marital void "drives" reconnection
RECOVERY	Can be immediate with forgiveness	Long-term process with marital therapy	Sobriety first; then individual therapy; later marital help	Long-term process with marital therapy
DURATION	One night	18–24 months	Years, with periods of binge behavior	Long-term with sporadic contact

COULD THIS BE YOU?

Though long and somewhat complicated, the following e-mail highlights many of the issues that make close calls so dangerous. Pay attention to the timing of the phone call, the dangerous partner's experience at this sort of behavior, the business stressors that set up this close call, the addiction that had long been an irritation in the marriage, and finally, the distance that made this new friendship "safe." Remember, no amount of miles will ever protect you in this culture!

Read this story in Gail's words:

"My husband, Garry, and I have been married for sixteen years. For the most part, our marriage has been happy. We owned and worked a business together for many years.

"About six years ago or so he was offered a position with our supplier. The offer was too good to pass up, and we both decided he should do it even though the plan had been for me to get out of running our business since I was becoming unfulfilled with it.

"I therefore remained at the helm of our business. As the years passed, I noticed our marriage starting to change. It started feeling more like a business relationship than a marriage since we would both try not to step on each other's toes taking care of the companies each of us were responsible for. One thing I seemed to notice was that Garry was more concerned about the company he was working for than the one he actually owned that I was overseeing, and this started to cause some ripples.

"Along with that complication, my husband has chewed tobacco ever since I met him. While we were dating, I had no problems with him chewing, as of course when you're dating, your guy has no faults! But as the years continued, I began to dislike the habit and the taste and smell it left in his mouth.

I began to kiss him less, and I let him know that that was why. We had gone to counseling a long time ago, and I brought that issue up, and he promptly told me in front of the counselor to live with his chewing. He had tried a few times to quit, but he seemed to go back to it pretty quickly.

"Around that time, we lost several of our business locations due to some 'political' reasons, and it was very difficult and emotional for both Garry and me. Since he did not have to work within our business on a daily basis as I did, he was able to get over the loss much more quickly. It affected me a lot, though. I felt I had lost half of my identity, yet Garry could not understand that. I do think it takes me longer to process things than he does.

"At any rate, our marriage began to suffer. We were also building a new home, and I was scared financially, especially since our business had just been cut in half. My husband does not worry about anything, so when I told him of my fears about going forward on the home, he pretty much said that he wanted to continue on and not to worry.

"We started to drift apart, and as we did, we started to argue and disagree, make demands on each other and give ultimatums. I kept asking him to quit chewing tobacco as I was tired of living with it, and it hurt me that he didn't love me enough to see how it affected me and my intimacy with him. He started complaining about lack of sex, and of course that made me feel unloved because he refused to even consider really trying to quit chewing. I also felt unloved because it seemed that my feelings on issues concerning the home we were building and so forth did not matter.

"A lady who worked for one of the vendors we used happened to call the day that Garry got the news about us losing the stores, and he told her the story. He said he felt something connected between the two of them. She lived clear across the country, and later that month she called Garry's secretary to have her e-mail a picture of him to her. She did! His secretary sent her a picture of him! Garry actually told me of this. He told me that he was very upset with his secretary for doing so, and therefore I felt that there was no threat.

"I guess over the next few months they began to call each other more often and talk on a personal level about things. Then Garry scheduled a business trip that allowed him to meet with her out of state. During this time, he and I drifted further apart. I asked him what was going on, told him I did not know him anymore, and had asked him if he was going through some sort of midlife crisis. I did ask him at one time if he was having an affair. His answer was 'When would I have time for an affair?' I had noticed his work hours got longer and longer, and he traveled more and more. When he was home, he'd arrive around 8:00 p.m. or so, eat dinner, then have an alcoholic drink, sit on the couch, and fall asleep within the hour.

"The weekend before he went to meet this woman, we had actually enjoyed a very fun and relaxing weekend together. We talked about our house that was starting, we dreamed together, we visited with family, we enjoyed each other. We did not argue or fight at all that weekend. He left Tuesday morning, kissed me, and said, 'I love you.' He called me later that evening and told me he loved me. Later I found out he called me from the lobby of the restaurant where he and his girlfriend were having dinner.

"What I didn't know was that he had packed three condoms in his suitcase for his trip.

"Not too long after that, I awoke early one morning to find my husband was already out of bed. I could see that he was in my office, so I got up to see what he was doing. He panicked when he saw me, like I had just caught him at something. I asked him what was up and he told me an unbelievable story, but I let it go. Later that morning, it bothered me, so I called him up and flat out asked him. He denied an affair at first; then I asked him if he was involved with or starting to have feelings for someone. The silence told me before he uttered the word *yes*.

"I then asked him what was going on, and he said he should come home. He told me about her but led me to believe that it was strictly a long-distance emotional type of thing, and he still refused to call it an affair. He told me his partial disclosure, turned my world upside down, then went and played golf with some attendees of a seminar that his work was putting on. He had promised that he'd play.

"We sought counseling. Over and over I asked if they had ever met and he denied it . . . in fact, he got angry that I kept asking. Then the American Express bill came in with a dinner for supposedly one person in the amount of $56. I questioned him, and he said he had broken up with her that night and was drinking and that was why the bill was so high. I actually contacted the restaurant and found that there were three meals on the ticket and not drinks (dinner was with him, her, and a friend of hers). I confronted him, and he said the restaurant sent the wrong receipt. Finally, several months later, I found out the truth. The woman's husband called me on my cell phone to tell me of the affair. I guess the husband had contacted Garry earlier that week and had been trying to contact me.

"We have sought counseling, but my husband does not really believe in it. He doesn't seem to realize the damage he caused by lying to me in the first place. He says he loves me and doesn't want her (he found out that she has had many affairs, had a sexual encounter with another man the night before they met, and had had an abortion behind her husband's back. He claims he found all of out this after they met in person).

"I want this to work out between Garry and me, but I really need him to find out why he did what he did."

DEVELOPMENT OF CLOSE CALLS

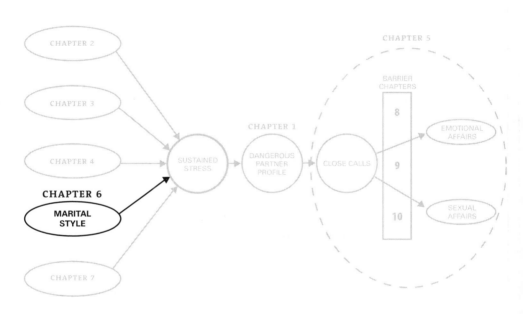

6 THE CLOSE CALL MARRIAGE:

Your Marital Style

Tom and Carol are the life of the party. They're both witty, sarcastic, and loads of fun to be with. They pick on each other, tease each other, and take jabs at each other, but always in a funny way. The trouble is, they don't just do that for an audience; they do it all the time at home. Those little zingers keep each away from the other. They don't get close out of fear of being hurt.

Chet and Betsy are just the opposite. They are the envy of the group in quite a different way. They never seem to disagree, much less actually fight, about anything. They seem to have the almost-perfect relationship. Some in the group have commented that their marriage appears too calm. They seem to know just what the other is thinking and anticipate each other's every need. Their home is so quiet, even with teenagers living in it.

Bob and Naomi are looked up to as having "made it." Their kids are all successful, and the last one is preparing to go off to college in just a few weeks. Their home was the one where all the teenagers wanted to hang out all the time. Noise was a way of life for them! They always took the greatest family vacations, and both parents were heavily involved in each of the children's after-school activities. Everyone in the group marveled at the energy they had put into raising their children.

What do these three marriages have in common, you ask? Each falls into a pattern at high risk for adultery, and if at risk for adultery, you can bet that they are at risk for a close call.

A question that has long intrigued those of us who work in the field of adultery recovery is, "Are some marital styles more prone to infidelity than others?"

The answer is yes. Now I hasten to say that just because your marital style might be in one of the high-risk categories doesn't mean that an affair lies in your future. However, it does mean that you and your spouse need to spend some time taking a look at this issue. If infidelity appears to cluster in these marital styles, then it goes without saying that these styles will have close calls.

As I review the marital styles that tend to have the higher incidents of close calls or even affairs, you and your spouse will have an opportunity to rate the prevalence of each style's characteristics in your marriage. Use a separate sheet of paper to tally your individual scores. There will also be some interesting discussion questions for the two of you. Again, remember no one's view is the "right one." Each of you is entitled to your own perception of your relationship. Be courageous. You need to be open, though, to your spouse's suggestions for improvements in the relationship.

MARITAL STYLES

Windshield Wiper

This first vulnerable marital style is one that avoids intimacy at all costs through constant bickering, criticism, demands, mean-spirited teasing, stated disappointments, and even open conflict. One spouse is always raising the bar, and the other spouse often feels like he or she never measures up. They would never separate — "Remember your vows" is the motto — but they do maintain an agreed-upon distance between them. They are like a set of windshield wipers — close in proximity, but always the same distance apart, never meeting, and therefore avoiding intimacy.

That distance is never discussed openly, but it is fully understood by both.

What may look like a terrible marriage to many outsiders is actually reassuring to the spouses. They feel safe because the relationship is so predictable. Though painful at times to both spouses, they still adhere to the marital rules. These spouses even test the system occasionally for no other reason than to see if they still receive the same response from the spouse that they did last time. Hurtful words are exchanged, and the same responses verify that all systems are in order. This is the couple where the spouse "pushes my buttons" or "yanks my chain." They will fight regularly over the same issues, never moving toward resolution. Remember, resolution is not the goal for this couple, just reassurance. That was Tom and Carol.

Not only does the conflict keep the spouses the right distance apart, it also contributes to a sense of power in both parties. They trade "tit for tat" as they volley back and forth. This balance of power is so critical that if one spouse has an affair, it is not unusual for the other spouse to have one also (to help the other "see what he/she did to me. Now we are equal").

Besides maintaining distance and keeping the power balanced, this windshield wiper relationship will allow the two spouses to carry out their family chores and assignments efficiently and without interference from each other. Note that when your car's windshield wipers clear the rain from your windshield, they don't clunk into each other (if they do, they are broken, and you promptly correct such close contact). Such a marriage relationship consists of two individuals who perform efficiently and predictably, stay the same distance apart, and even cover for one another, all the while seemingly held together (yet apart) by an invisible rod.

Often when one spouse begins to unbalance this marital style by suddenly receiving some sort of recognition, the other spouse will promptly find a new (or even an old) behavior to criticize and to bring the newly successful spouse back in line. Spouses in this marriage will counter any compliment they receive about their spouse with a complaint such as, "Oh, yes, they really are good at that, but you should see how they do this." Spouses in this marriage often see themselves as parental in certain areas, needing to finish the rearing of their oldest child—the spouse. They will often pick on their spouse and then say "Oh, I was just teasing." At times they can even humiliate their spouse in front of friends—anything to keep control of the relationship and to maintain the distance.

One young man I know was pained to hear his parents quarrelling when he was a child. When he became an adolescent, he sometimes intervened, trying to protect his mother from what he thought were the rages of his father. But to his utter amazement, his mother would turn on him and tell him to mind his own business—that she didn't need his help at all. In hindsight he realized that she was saying in effect, "Leave us alone; this is our dance. We are like two windshield wipers, furiously beating back and forth on the windshield, always the same distance apart. It is not really that bad."

Is this the style you see practiced in your marriage?

Look at the chart on the next page and select the number that reflects this tendency in your marriage: 1-never, 2-rarely, 3-sometimes, 4-often, 5-habitually. Make a copy so each of you can mark your selections on a separate sheet of paper.

THE WINDSHIELD WIPER CHARACTERISTICS

1–Never   2–Rarely   3–Sometimes   4–Often   5–Habitually

	1	2	3	4	5
Open conflict. Pick on each other, teasing					
Keep each other at arm's length					
Low-level nurturance in marital relationship					
Project oriented, looks efficient and effective					
If one partner does something (including infidelity), the other will also, to keep it "balanced"					
Push each other's buttons to "check out" if system is still intact					
Everything must look good to those outside the family					

Dial Tone

Whereas the previous marital style resembles the windshield wipers on your automobile, this kind of relationship could best be described as the dial tone on your landline phone. Like the dial tone, there is no variation; it is always predictable, and conflict is neatly avoided. That is initially reassuring, but it can be maddening when you listen to it for long periods of time. Just try holding the receiver to your ear for a while — you will see what I mean.

Individuals in this relationship will either have separate roles, lifestyles, and interests, or one spouse will run everything while the other spouse becomes an obedient child. In the former case, the two mates have very rigid roles that don't intermingle well. Both know exactly what to do, and it does no good to argue for a different procedure. Everything is predictable — maddeningly so. There's no need to argue, as Chet and Betsy discovered . . . but drudgery and lifelessness result.

In these relationships, one partner is often the powerful one who will make the family good, but it is "peace at any price" and therefore decidedly unhealthy. Sometimes one partner is the parent and the other the child. For example:

- She puts all the food on his plate because "He won't eat right unless I put it in front of him."
- He gives her an allowance like he gives the children, "Because she doesn't know how to handle money."
- She buys all of his clothes, picks out what he is to wear, and packs his suitcase, because "He doesn't know how to dress himself."
- He takes her everywhere because "It is dangerous for her to drive on the freeways."

Unfortunately, such conflict avoidance is common among Christians. The emphasis placed on looking good in many evangelical circles encourages couples to believe in a false serenity; they misinterpret the dial tone as smooth sailing. Many people use this kind of marriage as a "Christian example" for others to emulate, but it is missing a large ingredient of life — the ability to treat each other with mutual respect and to be human and honest with yourself, others, and God.[1]

(The appendix of this book contains some guidelines on communication and conflict resolution. These ideas are designed to get you started talking and *listening*!)

Interestingly, both partners usually appear content with the dial tone arrangement, but that can change quickly when one begins to feel the close call attraction to the dangerous partner. Suddenly a whole new range of emotions becomes available to the infatuated one. A new awareness of being alive surfaces; the freedom from the dial tone is exhilarating; the transformation within is unbelievably wonderful. Should an infatuation happen in this kind of marriage, the spouse will often say, "I don't even know this person. I have never seen him act like this. He has never shown this kind of behavior in our marriage."

The marital deficit in this kind of marriage is often very difficult for either spouse to recognize. It was a "perfect" relationship, and the feeling is often that "I was a perfect spouse" in the marriage. Spouses in this kind of marriage often think that to change would mean admitting "I was making a mistake." To acknowledge that would devastate the reputation that each spouse had worked so hard to build. Often a spouse in this marital style has lots of support from within the church family and finds it easy to maintain their reputation while holding the newly infatuated spouse totally responsible for what might be happening. In reality, both spouses have contributed to the deterioration of the marriage, and into this boring relationship can come a close call.

Is this your style? Look over the Dial Tone Characteristics chart. Again, make a copy so you can each mark your papers separately.

THE DIAL TONE CHARACTERISTICS

1–Never   2–Rarely   3–Sometimes   4–Often   5–Habitually

	1	2	3	4	5
Little disagreement, no conflict allowed					
No differences tolerated, "look alike"					
Fixed, efficient roles for everyone in the family					
Tendency to be enmeshed, put off outside attachments					
Look perfect and do everything together or not at all					
Very little emotion, especially anger, expressed					
Parent-child relationship between spouses					

Empty Nest

An individual in this type of marriage who has a close call is typically the conscientious family man and/or the perfect mother. He or she has put in twenty years or more of parenting. Once the kids have gone there's little left to talk about. All the unfinished business (unresolved issues) of their own families of origin, all the stuff they have left undone in their marriage because there was always more to do than anyone had time for, comes pushing to the forefront. Combine those factors with the unknowns of the future, and you have a situation where both are vulnerable to the affection, attention, and nurturance of the dangerous partner person.

This couple often starts their marriage highly committed to providing their children with the emotional nurturance they may never have received in their families of origin. They dedicate all their time, money, and energy to providing the "great family experience." These are the parents who are involved in everything that touches their children's lives, whether it's home-schooling or being involved with their school's PTA, to being band parents, Sunday school teachers, soccer moms, fund-raiser coordinators, to coaching the sports teams.

All of this is admirable, except that the marital relationship can atrophy and die a slow death while the family relationship is blossoming. This deterioration is so slow that neither spouse is aware that distance is growing between them. They are too busy to even think of "us." Besides, it would seem selfish to spend "family money" on any "couple fun." They function beautifully, are overly responsible, and neither would ever think the other is unhappy until one of them has a close call.

Remember the dangerous partner from chapter 1? When the dangerous partner crosses their field of vision, their resistance often collapses immediately. They've been exhausted and had no idea how needy they were. Neither spouse has had the time to nurture the other. They are starved for adult affection and care.

Now complete the Empty Nest Pattern chart and see how your marriage is doing in this area.

EMPTY NEST PATTERN

1–Never   2–Rarely   3–Sometimes   4–Often   5–Habitually

	1	2	3	4	5
Sacrificial, heroic support of and focus on the children					
The marriage feels empty, boring, quiet					
Little effort and money spent to maintain a marriage					
No dating, and sex is perfunctory					
Satisfaction derived from family happiness					
Awareness of spousal emptiness surfaces when children begin to depart					
View each other as a great parent, not as a lovable spouse					

Does one of these styles describe your marriage more than another? Where did you score highest on your patterns of interactions? What do you like about these patterns? What don't you like? And how have you contributed to the development of this pattern in your marriage? Where might you have seen this pattern practiced?

PATTERNS OF ANGER, POWER, CONTROL

Anger

Every family has its own way of dealing with anger, and every family has patterns of power play.

What practices did you experience in your family of origin? For example, what were the "rules"? Look at the suggestions below and see which, if any, reflect the common practices you grew up with.

- Some families run away from anger entirely, lest they say something they will later regret.

- Some family members can only be verbal with anger, while others can physically hit people or things. Some members are allowed to knock holes in the walls or slam doors.

- Some families have different rules for the males and females in the family.

- Some families "select" one person to be angry all the time — to express the anger for everyone else in the family.

- Some families say, in effect, "Smile, everything's fine."

- Some families behave as though conflict doesn't bother them but retaliate when another least expects it.

Is there a pattern of managing anger that you recognize here? Was it consistent all the time you lived with this family? Who enforced the practices and how? Was any family member free from the rules that controlled all the others?

Now that you've thought about these things, consider this: How have you brought/let your family of origin's anger management practice into your marriage? Does it work here? Is your spouse satisfied? What, if anything, needs to change?

Power and Control

Rules of power and control are not, of course, written on the bulletin board in the kitchen. No family member gets a star after his or her name for following these practices! But these practices are just as real as though they were etched in the wall.

Give some thought to who held power in your family of origin and how that control played out. To get you thinking, consider these:

- What role did each of your parents play in the family interaction?
- What role did each of your siblings play?
- What role did you play?
- Did you ever wish things were different when you were a child?
- Who had the most power in your family?
- How did that person maintain it?
- How has this influenced you?
- Are you practicing these same patterns with your family—your spouse, your children?
- Are there things in your present pattern you'd like to change?

In the next chapter, we'll look at some more aspects of your marital style, concentrating on interactions and patterns you might not have been aware of. Through this process of examination, taking apart, and putting together, the two of you can change your ways to better reflect your long-term desires, new growth, and intimacy.

COULD THIS BE YOU?

The following account is so heartfelt, so contrite, told with such anguish, that it really doesn't need an introduction. The progression of this close call is evident to everyone. This is a story of a man who got swept away even though he thought he was strong enough to swim against the current of this attraction . . . but you can't, you won't, and you don't. Read Devin's story.

"I am really struggling with how this could happen to me when I sincerely didn't want it to happen.

"When my 'partner' first expressed her feelings to me, I tried to get her to join me in a discussion with our boss. She steadfastly refused—I only wish I had insisted.

"At the time I thought I could control the situation on my own. For months I counseled her about emotional problems she was dealing with and kept telling her that an affair between us was not going to happen. Even when my resolve began to wane, I prayed with her. I prayed for God to take this temptation away from us. I prayed to God to bless and protect our spouses and our children. I prayed to God for guidance and direction to help us.

"Of course, I knew what to do—get up and run away as fast as I could. Oh, how I wished I would have. Still it troubles me greatly that this happened, and that I somehow allowed this to happen, that God let it happen when I prayed to Him earnestly for help.

"Why? Why did this have to happen to me? I am a good person who has never done anything like this in my life. Why did God allow this to happen? Was it a test I failed? Was it an attack of Satan? Was it my own weakness even though I have never had this problem before?

"All my life I have been a man of strong moral conviction. This just deepens my shame."

NOTE

1. For ideas on learning the difference between attacks that hurt and tactics that heal, see *Fight Fair!* by Tim and Joy Downs (Chicago: Moody, 2004).

DEVELOPMENT OF CLOSE CALLS

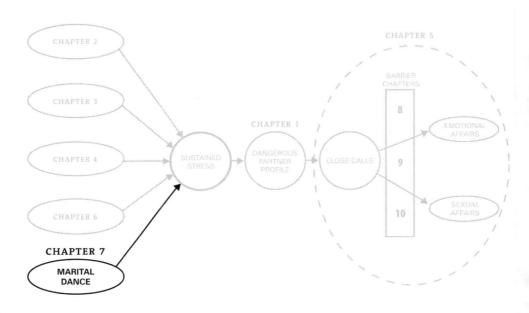

7 THE CLOSE CALL VACUUM:
Your Marital Dance

"How was your day?" June asked when Matt came home.

"Fine. Traffic was bad. How was work?" he asked in return.

"Good enough. Two meetings, not productive, but that's how they usually are."

"I know what you mean. Any mail?"

"Junk mostly. It's on the desk."

Safe. A safe conversation. Matt and June knew what they could talk about, what was their marital dance, what were their focal points, how they interacted. Keep it safe.

But was that enough?

I was recently counseling Matt and June, who had come to my office for help with serious problems in their marriage. Since it was my first time meeting with them,

I asked a lot of questions and occasionally made a comment or two. Somewhere in that hour, I observed, "It sounds like you two have been disappointed with your marriage and angry with each other for years."

Matt said, "I've been trying to tell her that since the first year we were married. She refused to believe me." Well, now that they're in the counselor's office, June believes him.

What happened? How could this couple have missed connecting with each other almost from the beginning? Like many couples, Matt and June hadn't examined what each brought to the marriage. The result was frustration and anger. For some couples, the result is boredom and resignation.

Remember the Moon-Earth analogy in chapter 1? That's when we come to settle for that side of the moon — or spouse — that we can see and don't explore the other side. Well, here is a series of activities that will allow you to explore your mate's other side and allow you to expose yours.

Have some fun going through this chapter — you'll find it quite interesting! Talk only about yourself and stay away from using the word *you*. Listen attentively to each other. Build on what you learn here with the information you gleaned in the last chapter about your marital style.

In this chapter, you will look at your:

- Marital focal point
- Marital dance
- Marital contributions
- Marital opposites
- Marital behaviors
- Marital patterns influenced by parents' marriage

EXAMINING YOUR WAYS

Marital Focal Point

Every marriage has some items that consume the conversation much of the time, while other topics are off-limits for discussion. When couples have alone time, they will inherently choose to talk about the safe topics. If you are not careful, that cluster of safety will become the *only* things the two of you will talk about, and your relationship will become boring. Identify the issues that belong in the following categories and see if you can both agree to talk about some things that have been difficult in the past.

How would each of you answer these questions?

- When we talk, we only talk about:
- I try to talk about:
- We can't talk about:

Marital Dance

Similar to and involved with the previous activity, the following material highlights the "dance" that often perpetuates disappointments in the marriage. Couples often develop point/counterpoint responses that do not solve anything. Here are some examples:

- When he questions why I spent money a certain way, I withdraw and do the silent treatment.
- When she doesn't want to have sex, and I do, I sulk.
- When he/she makes comments about my being late, I ignore that issue and come back with all the bad things he/she does.

Sound familiar? Be honest here and make a list, the longer the better. That pulls your dance out into the open where you can together identify changes you want to make.

When my spouse _____, I _____.

When my spouse _____, I _____.

When my spouse _____, I _____.

Marital Contributions

As you continue to uncover your marital style, determine the contributions each of you makes to the marriage. Some examples might be, "I provide all the money; she provides all the spending." Or, "I provide all the housework; he provides all the TV watching." Of course, I'm teasing here a little bit, but this section highlights the feelings of unfairness that often pervade marriages prior to close calls. Remember, you're listening to each other, and the idea is to enjoy working through this, not enter a blame game!

I provide all the _____.

My spouse provides all the _____.

I provide all the _____.

My spouse provides all the _____.

I provide all the _____.

My spouse provides all the _____.

Marital Opposites

Opposites do attract, and nowhere is this more obvious than in marriages. Ironically, it is often true that a personality trait, initially attractive to a spouse, later turns out to be one of the chief irritants between them. Examples here would include "I am punctual; he is late." Or, "I am fun-loving, but she is too busy for downtime."

I am _____, my spouse is _____.

I am _____, my spouse is _____.

I am _____, my spouse is _____.

Marital Behaviors

Here I identify behaviors that help and hurt marital intimacy — the kind of soul-mate bonding we all desire yet so few of us enjoy. List the behaviors that bring you closer and that drive you apart. I provide only three work spaces for these paired behaviors, but if you find more in your relationship, by all means use additional paper. Examples might include: "We get close when I initiate sex; we move apart when I want to just talk." Or, "We get close when I buy you flowers; we move apart when I watch football all weekend."

Remember, these are only "I" statements — no fair using "you"!

We get close when I _____;

we move apart when I _____.

We get close when I _____;

we move apart when I _____.

We get close when I _____;

we move apart when I _____.

Well, you should know more about your marital style now than you did before. You've identified and highlighted items where you see opportunity to change, expand, and grow.

You will have multiple opportunities to discuss these with your spouse. Add these items to those topics that are never off-limits.

This has been a fairly complex examination. However, most couples who do this work find it incredibly enlightening.

Before we move on, here's a new challenge for the two of you: Name the patterns that have emerged. Make up a code phrase that either of you can use to identify slippage back into old patterns. Don't accuse your spouse of doing the old behavior by saying, "You just did . . ." Instead, agree that when you or your spouse reverts to a pattern you both wanted to avoid, say something like, "I think there's a squirrel in here."

Marital Patterns Influenced by Parents' Marriage

Are you familiar with the comic *Cathy*? In one insightful strip, Cathy's mother is telling her how she should organize her coupons, sort her mail, and so on. Cathy says dismissively, "I have my own system, Mother." Later in a store, her friend says, "Here's a good brand of detergent." Cathy rejects it, wailing, "That's not the kind my mother buys!"

We've already talked about some family of origin issues, and how much influence these have on your life and marriage. Beyond that, many do not realize how much influence the way your parents *interacted* has on your own marriage. You might even be imitating their behavior subconsciously, expecting a certain response from your spouse, when, in fact, your actions guarantee a response that is not what you were expecting.

Take a few minutes and clarify the patterns you saw your parents practice across several different areas of their relationship. Some of you might be thinking, *I have no idea*! If that's the case, ask a sibling, an aunt, or your parents directly.

Take a look at the areas shown below—add any others you think of—and consider how they played out in your parents' marriage. Make some notes, reflect back on specific circumstances, and talk about this information with your spouse.

- Displays of affection
- Husband/wife roles
- Attitudes displayed about sex
- Issues with children
- Communication patterns
- Power/control issues
- Manipulations/means of influence each used
- Conflict/anger/differences between them
- Money patterns
- Nurturance/fun

When you and your spouse talk about these things, remember that you're describing your parents' behavior; use the linkage "and as a result in my marriage, I tend to . . . "

Now that your thinking about how your parents' interactions patterns have affected your own marriage, look at the chart called "Parental Influence in Our Marriage." Jot down who had the primary responsibilities for the various areas given in your families of origin and in your marriage. How satisfied are you and your spouse (5 is high) with the patterns you're practicing? On your own worksheet, each of you will guess how satisfied your spouse is with the pattern.

This is a good time to think and discuss what you like and don't like about this interaction pattern. Think back to when you saw it practiced, or modeled, before you met your spouse, and why you might be maintaining this pattern even though you don't like it.

PARENTAL INFLUENCE IN OUR MARRIAGE

As you fill out this review, remember the purpose is to share it with your spouse face-to-face. Only jot notes sufficient to remind you of what you want to share. Keep in mind that many marital interactions are a response to or a reaction against what one experienced in their family of origin. The issue is not "is this a good or bad practice?" but rather, "are we both happy with it, or are we just behaving this way because our parents did/did not do it this way?"

	Primary Responsibility		My Own Satisfaction	Spouse's
BEHAVIOR ROLES	Family of origin	Marriage	Rate: 1 2 3 4 5	Rate: 1 2 3 4 5
Cars			1 2 3 4 5	1 2 3 4 5
Housecleaning			1 2 3 4 5	1 2 3 4 5
Household chores			1 2 3 4 5	1 2 3 4 5
Cooking/menus/ food purchases			1 2 3 4 5	1 2 3 4 5
Child care			1 2 3 4 5	1 2 3 4 5
Home maintenance			1 2 3 4 5	1 2 3 4 5
Yard maintenance			1 2 3 4 5	1 2 3 4 5
Remodeling/decorating			1 2 3 4 5	1 2 3 4 5
Bills/financial mgmt.			1 2 3 4 5	1 2 3 4 5
SCHEDULES				
Who gets up first			1 2 3 4 5	1 2 3 4 5
Who gets to stay up late			1 2 3 4 5	1 2 3 4 5
Who gets up first with children			1 2 3 4 5	1 2 3 4 5
Who makes sure home is secure			1 2 3 4 5	1 2 3 4 5
Who gets to sleep in			1 2 3 4 5	1 2 3 4 5
Who gets to enjoy their hobbies first			1 2 3 4 5	1 2 3 4 5
Whose friends matter most in family schedules			1 2 3 4 5	1 2 3 4 5

VALUES	Primary Responsibility		My Own Satisfaction	Spouse's
	Family of origin	Marriage	Rate: 1 2 3 4 5	Rate: 1 2 3 4 5
Who spends money			1 2 3 4 5	1 2 3 4 5
Who saves money			1 2 3 4 5	1 2 3 4 5
Who has most discretionary income			1 2 3 4 5	1 2 3 4 5
WHO IS RESPONSIBLE FOR				
Family spirituality			1 2 3 4 5	1 2 3 4 5
Couple closeness			1 2 3 4 5	1 2 3 4 5
Sex			1 2 3 4 5	1 2 3 4 5
Family activities			1 2 3 4 5	1 2 3 4 5
Family scheduling / shuttling of children			1 2 3 4 5	1 2 3 4 5
Relationships / atmosphere			1 2 3 4 5	1 2 3 4 5
Children's homework			1 2 3 4 5	1 2 3 4 5

1. Items where I follow my Family of Origin (FOR) practices:

2. Items where I do the opposite of my FOR:

3. Items I wish we would practice now like my FOR:

4. My impressions after looking over my responses:

5. My impressions after sharing with my spouse:

This entire discussion highlights what the Judeo-Christian Scriptures have required of married couples for over six thousand years: Leave your mother and father, and cleave to your spouse.[1] The two of you have to establish your own patterns. You are both free to create what you have always wanted. You don't have to do marriage the way your parents or your culture pressures you to. Make your marriage your own.

COULD THIS BE YOU?

Having just spent some time looking at your marital style, you'll have no problem identifying the style of the couple in the story below. Their story readily highlights much of what *Close Calls* has described to this point: the dangerous partner, the close calls characteristics, the family of origin risk factors, the marital interactions, the environmental stressors and triggers, the decline of marital satisfaction, and the addictions necessary to manage the pain.

Remember, nobody sets out to deliberately do this to their most important relationship on earth. Manny and Dinah have taken some time to lay out their story for us. I have let them tell it in their own unedited words; their experience reminds us that this can happen to almost anyone given the right cluster of what Manny calls "the perfect storm" of contributing factors.

Manny: "We have learned much about what went horribly wrong in our marriage. Like the title of an epic disaster film, our 20-year marriage was hit by 'the perfect storm' of contributing factors. Although we were deeply in love, high school sweethearts, and best friends, our unresolved issues, poor communications, and hurt feelings dragged our marriage down to a point where it was inevitable that one of us would have an affair.

"We both came from broken families with adulterous

fathers. Our own parents were poor role models for a strong marriage. We both had lost a parent to early death, and neither of us had really taken the time to grieve those losses. We battled each other on how to raise our children, how to spend our money, and even on how to decorate our home. We had opposite styles of expression. I was loud and wore my feelings on the outside while Dinah was quiet and stuffed her feelings deep down.

"Hurt feelings drove us apart and intimacy began to fade. Our sex life was robust, but it lacked the beauty of a spiritual oneness. We were involved in ministry three or four nights a week, but spiritually we were dying inside.

"Aching from a lack of intimacy, I sought solace in a secret addiction to Internet porn.

"In the midst of our deteriorating marriage, we began to spend more and more time with another family in our church. For lack of strong family ties in our immediate family, our friends became our adopted family. We regularly shared meals, vacations, celebrating birthdays and holidays. Dinah considered Tammy to be her best friend, and I considered Paul my best friend. We confided much in each other and personal boundaries were fairly weak.

"Eventually, I realized my anger and porn addiction were out of control. I needed help. I turned to Paul and another friend to hold me accountable. For several months they met with me as I worked through a strong moral inventory. They prayed for me. At the end of that time, we scheduled a meeting with Dinah so I could confess my porn addiction and to ask forgiveness for my abusive speech and behaviors. Paul and the other friend now knew all of the intimate details of my personal struggles and of the struggles within our marriage."

Dinah: "I was hurt by Manny's revelations and in some ways feeling justified in my own past poor behaviors, without as yet even understanding just how much I had contributed to the cycle of anger our marriage had become. I loved my husband and understood that he was working hard at making things right. I expressed my willingness to forgive him but was really completely clueless as to what my real feelings in the situation were. I had been taught throughout my life to do and say the right things and to stuff personal feelings away. So I said the right words and let the feelings of hurt, anger, and loneliness stew.

"Paul's marriage was also in the midst of big struggles at this point. In fact, Paul and his wife had been going to marriage counseling for a number of months. Awhile after that confession meeting, Paul called me and asked if I would meet him for lunch so that he could talk with me about his struggles and perhaps get a woman's insight into the issues he and Tammy were facing. Manny allowed me to go to that lunch meeting, although he had some misgivings about its appropriateness.

"Paul and I met a few times for lunch chats, all but the first without Manny's knowledge. Tammy had no knowledge of any of this. I admired Paul's calm, never-angry manner of speech, his apparent patience with his wife, and his ability to listen to my frustrations without judgment. He was easy to talk to and seemed genuinely interested in what I had to say on any subject.

"During those lunches the topic remained Paul's marriage but began to include the issues in mine as well. Because he already knew the details of my own marriage, he could easily draw parallels between their struggles and ours. These meetings didn't go on indefinitely. They soon ended, but the seeds of both inappropriate intimacy and deception were planted. At this point, I still had no inclination that the relationship would go any further.

"Since I was eighteen, I have had occasional migraine

headaches. Some months prior to the actual beginning of the affair, I developed a chronic headache and was waking up each day in pain and managing the pain throughout the day with over-the-counter painkillers. About once a month, the headache developed into a full-blown migraine and I ended up in the emergency room.

"One weekend when Manny was out of the state for business, I developed one of these migraines while the kids and I were at Paul and Tammy's house. Paul took me to the emergency room and was very supportive and comforting during the wait to see the doctor. He held on to me as I rocked in pain in the waiting room and rubbed my head after I was taken into a room. I didn't think anything more of this than being grateful for the physical care. In his mind, he had crossed a line from being attracted to me (I was as yet blind to this) to wanting more from the relationship. I know now that his taking me was a mistake in and of itself. It put both of us in an emotionally vulnerable place.

"A couple of weeks later, Paul asked to see me. When we talked, he expressed his love and attraction for me. I acknowledged that I cared for him as well, but not in the same way. I had allowed him, and not his wife or my husband, to become my 'best friend.' I felt valued in that relationship. I had never thought about a physical attraction to him, but finding myself in that situation, I easily slipped into looking at him in that new way. On that day, I did not believe that the relationship would go any further. I knew it would be wrong. But I foolishly thought it could stay the way it was, when the way it was had already begun the downward spiral out of control. Within days we saw each other again and began the physical relationship that was inevitable.

"At first these meetings were exciting. I felt like the sexual relationship was just a further dimension of what was a loving, caring friendship. It didn't take long for me to begin emotionally crashing. I met with Paul and enjoyed that time, but by the time I got home I was an emotional wreck of guilt and remorse. But, back again I went when he called. I was addicted to the attention he paid me intellectually and emotionally and was willing to accept the sexual relationship to maintain friendship. All this time, we as couples were as close as ever. The physical relationship lasted on and off for two years. At one point I couldn't go on and called an end to that aspect of our affair.

"Paul said that he would honor that but he didn't want to. He persisted in calling me, asking me to meet him for lunch, which I did. I knew this was wrong, but still enjoyed the conversation and didn't know how to end it and yet maintain all of our friendships. I was delusional to think that we could get beyond what had happened and get back to a couples friendship.

"Within a few months, an event happened that brought a suspicion of the affair to light in the church. When confronted by one of the pastors, I denied the affair. At that point I became suicidal. I was scared enough of these feelings to go to my doctor and ask for help in the form of medication. He thankfully would not give me anything but spent about an hour talking to me. He convinced me that the best way to deal with what was happening was head-on.

I told Manny the truth that night and begged his forgiveness. I wanted my marriage to work and was willing to endure whatever I had to from Manny to get to a place of healing. I had no idea what form that was going to take."

Manny: "Dinah's revelation was the shock of my life. I was devastated. The man I considered my dearest friend, my closest confidant, had betrayed me in the worst possible way. He had used the knowledge of my sins to denigrate me before my wife and woo her away, all the while pretending to care for me. He later admitted that his 'friendship' was simply a ruse to account for my whereabouts and to glean useful information to paint me in a worse light before my wife.

"For the first time in my life I understood personal rage. Thoughts of revenge and even murder ran through my head. My self-esteem was destroyed, and I had suicidal feelings. The agony was unbearable.

"My gossip-ridden church only made matters worse. In order to prevent our children hearing of their mother's shame from a Sunday school classmate, we were forced to preempt such a tragedy and tell them the truth ourselves. The destruction of that knowledge was a brutal blow to such tender hearts. Eventually, our family left our church and moved to a new church. I left behind almost all my friendships developed over decades of fellowship.

"Although I verbally forgave my wife the night of her confession, the actual act of forgiveness took years to accomplish. Each new fact that came to light had to be processed and forgiven. For nearly two years, visual reminders of the affair attacked me daily, triggering feelings of revulsion and depression.

"In addition to my own pain, I often had to carry the load of my wife's sorrow. Her friends abandoned her, her spiritual leaders condemned her, and her children struggled to trust her. As I struggled to rebuild my own trust for her, I was often her only support."

Dinah: "I hate that Manny and I have had to go through this whole process. I hate that I brought this ugly chapter into our lives. But God's grace is an amazing healer. Our marriage was not just healed from the sin of adultery; our marriage was restored and strengthened into what is now a joyous thing.

"The process of healing was painful. For two to three

years I agonized through Manny's rages. My heart broke for the pain he was going through, and my body suffered with the depression and anxiety I was living with, but I was committed to enduring whatever was needed to get through that process. I have no regrets about confessing to my husband and asking for his forgiveness. The gift he gave me of working hard to battle through the devastation he experienced without walking away from me was enormous.

"I had to deal with daily personal shame and guilt, many days not knowing if I would ever feel forgiven, ever again feel any self-forgiveness or any self-respect. When I looked in the mirror, all I saw was my shame.

"Now, five years to the month of my confession to Manny, I can say with all honesty, I am glad to have gone through this process. Adultery and recovery is certainly not a path I would recommend to heal a marriage, but it is the path we were on, and by God's grace we walked it together. I have found my true family in Manny. He is my heart and the love of my life."

NOTE
1. See Genesis 2:24.

SECTION 3:
Barriers to Close Call Development

BARRIERS TO CLOSE CALLS

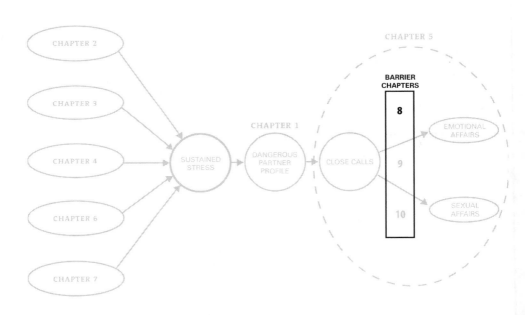

8 ATTITUDES:
Exterior and Interior

DON AND CHRISTY

"I was wrong when I let the vet put your dog to sleep," began Don's forgiveness letter.

Ten years earlier, when he and Christy were planning to marry, she had asked if she could bring her childhood dog into their marriage. Her parents did not want to keep it any longer, and it was quite aged and ill. Since they were going to be living in the same town in which Christy had grown up, and as a result the dog could continue to see the same veterinarian who had always cared for it, Don said yes.

Soon into the marriage, Christy left for a major business trip to the East Coast. Sure enough, the dog became ill and, as the dutiful husband, Don took Crackers to the family vet. The doctor, after examination, said it was time to put Crackers to sleep. It was unkind to try to keep him alive any longer. The disease had progressed to the point that all the vet could offer was sedation.

Don wasn't about to let the vet do this until Christy had a say in what she wanted done. He tried all day to reach her without success. Finally, just before 6:00 p.m. that evening, still unable to reach his wife, he called the vet and shared his predicament. The vet responded, "I have known your wife since she was eight years old, and I have cared for this dog since he was six weeks old. It is best to put Crackers to sleep. When Christy gets back in town, have her call me, and I'll explain everything to her."

Well, you can imagine what happened. When Christy came home, Crackers was gone, and she had never had a chance to say good-bye to her childhood pet. That event started an insidious inability to completely trust her husband. Even though he had tried to do his best, this experience planted doubt in Christy's mind that Don genuinely had her best interests in mind.

The seed that whispered to Christy that Don was untrustworthy took root and grew, fed by other incidents over the years that should have been of little account. But now, some ten years later, Christy had succumbed to a close call and had gotten involved with someone at work. Though hurt and angry, and feeling unjustly blamed again, Don was man enough to recognize that some of this mistrust had its roots in his earlier experience of not standing up for Christy's best interests.

FORGIVENESS

One of the most influential vulnerabilities to close calls is the inability to let go, to forgive, and to work through old hurts and wounds in the marriage. Both Don and Christy felt justified in hanging on to the individual hurt and anger the incident with Crackers had caused. Both felt the other was to blame. Both felt misunderstood, but with the passage of time, both became distracted, and this little hurt went underground—unforgiven and unaddressed.

Every marriage has these kinds of hurts, but it is their cumulative effect that makes one vulnerable to a close call. It is easy to see how their buildup can create the feeling that "He doesn't really care about me," or "she is too interested in everybody else, including the kids." Now some would dismiss small isolated events and say that he just needs to grow up or she just needs to quit complaining. These things may well be true, but most adulterers can recount long histories of small disappointments in their marriage relationship.

For years, I tried to figure out how to help couples protect themselves from this vulnerability. But finally, as I continued to listen to Don recount his forgiveness letter, I said, "Eureka! This is the answer." After Don made the initial statement of wrongdoing, he said, "I know this caused you to feel betrayed and unprotected by me." That was what turned out to be the key for Christy to be able to forgive him. In this case, all he had to do was acknowledge how she felt and how his behavior affected her emotionally. Once he was able to do that (on his own, I might add, without any coaching from me), she was able to let go of that long-standing hurt. Upon hearing him acknowledge her injury, she immediately burst into tears and acknowledged how bitter she had become toward him over the loss of Crackers.

Here are some ways we can respond to hurts we all experience in our marriages:

One way is to overlook the offense. Most of us will ignore something initially or even complain about it occasionally, but overall we let it slide. In this scenario, it continues to grow but it moves away from our awareness. You might talk to yourself about it; you might even offer excuses why your spouse does this, but most of us realize we have to pick our battles carefully. You can't fight about everything and still have a relationship. No one is perfect, and you know your mate has lots of good qualities.[1] But this little hurt added to others starts to accumulate, and now it is influencing some of your responses to your spouse. It changes your attitude. It creates its own emotional distance. It makes you settle for less than you want in the relationship. It can make you vulnerable to attention from someone else.

Another response is to recognize that this is the kind of stuff that, over time, often causes one spouse to say to the other, "We need counseling." You can go that way, and in many cases it's quite helpful. It takes time and a commitment on each spouse's part.

There are also lots of weekend retreats, enrichment conferences, self-help guides, and many fine books, all of which can have a good effect on the relationship. But many of these fail to address the old accumulated hurts and choose to address instead the current interaction patterns of the marriage. I support all of the options, but there is a choice that is free, but often underutilized by couples.

Forgiveness History

Though it sounds simple, the practice of forgiveness is really a complex behavior that is greatly influenced by each spouse's individual experience with personal forgiveness. Forgiveness is a learned skill. The ability to forgive is shaped by your history with it.

Think about these questions and talk about them together:

- What has been my overall experience with forgiveness?
- Have I been easily forgiven?
- Do I forgive easily?
- When I have been hurt, have those who hurt me quickly identified their wrongdoing and corrected their behavior?

▨ What was my family of origin's pattern of apology and forgiveness?

▨ Are there people who need my forgiveness? Are there people I need to ask forgiveness of?

▨ What are some of my misgivings about the process of forgiveness?

Writing a Letter

In this age of e-mails and texting, perhaps you haven't written a letter in a very long time! But there's something powerful in the written word, and if you and your spouse will write a forgiveness letter, you will have a tangible memento of the time when you decided to deal with old hurts and move on.

As we've said, virtually every marriage has some buildup of undealt with and unforgiven issues. And most of us need help in identifying our part in this buildup. There are generally three areas in which this occurs:

First—things you did in the marriage that you should not have done. This isn't a time to justify your behavior, just to take responsibility for it.

Second—things that you didn't do that you should have done. In this arena are all the behaviors that we know are necessary for good relationships, but due to circumstances—our spouse's behavior, our own weaknesses, and so forth—we become stubborn and refuse to act appropriately.

Third—(and this is the tough area) is a category I call "Accidental." This is where things just happen, like what happened to Don at the beginning of the chapter when he allowed the vet to put Crackers to sleep. He wasn't trying to do anything but make the best choice, and he felt obligated to follow the advice of the expert.

Other examples of this might be the husband who finds himself with a tyrannical boss or caught in the midst of a company buyout over which he has little or no control. Wives can often find themselves caught up in the care of a chronically ill child, taking care of aging parents, or having their own physical limitations caused by illness. None of these experiences would be anyone's first choice, but they dictate things like behavior, schedules, and finances in ways that can be quite injurious to a marriage. Just stand up and say that you were wrong in letting this (whatever it is) rob you and your spouse of time together and identify how these uncontrollable matters must have made your spouse feel. Identifying these "accidentals" and your response to them doesn't make you a bad person—quite the opposite! And your spouse will not use this against you, as you will not use your spouse's against him or her.

What you are going to do is just work on the first part: Identify what you have contributed to the marriage that has been injurious to the relationship and to your spouse.

Write your behavior (without defending yourself in any way) following the words:

- "I was wrong when I . . ."
- "I know this must have made you feel . . ."
- "Will you forgive me?"

(To assist you in this process, refer to the Feeling Words chart found in the appendix.)

In order to facilitate forgiveness, you should list the items from "least offensive" to the "most offensive." Remember, you are doing this activity to receive some forgiveness. Start with the items that will be the easiest for your spouse to forgive.

I know you might be thinking, "What if my spouse doesn't want to do this?" Remember, forgiveness is never based on reciprocal action. No matter what the other person does, you are called to acknowledge your own behavior. Ideally, your spouse will engage in this process, but if he or she chooses not to, that is still no justification for you not to acknowledge what you have done wrong. Take the initiative. You will feel better, and you'll be a better person for having done it.

Now, just before you finish writing your letter, you might want to try this: Place an empty chair in front of you. Pretend your spouse is sitting in that empty chair, and sit down so you can "look" at him or her. "Show" your completed forgiveness letter and "ask" if there is anything else that should be in this letter that you need to ask forgiveness for. Be still and quietly reflect on this process. Remember, this is a pivotal opportunity to take care of old business, so you want to do it thoroughly.

If your spouse has agreed to do this forgiveness exercise with you, then set aside a minimum of a half an hour with no interruptions to read your letters to each other. You will also need some downtime after the reading to reflect on what you both have heard and read. Prior to reading the letters, read through the following instructions together. Discuss and make sure that you agree on them prior to the reading process.

Requesting and Giving Forgiveness

- Decide who will start.
- Sit facing each other, close enough to touch each other.
- Read slowly and read only what is written. Do not ad-lib.
- Make eye contact as often as possible, especially at the last phrase of each item when you ask for forgiveness.
- When listening, each of you is free to ask your spouse to reread any item in the letter. (Sometimes it is cleansing just to hear your spouse acknowledge a shortcoming that has hurt you for years.)
- On occasion, a spouse will correctly identify a wrong behavior but misidentify the feelings that the

behavior generated in their spouse. If that happens, the hearer should say to the one reading the letter, "I want to talk about the feelings later." You will have a chance to clarify the feelings in the next part of the exercise, but don't discuss it now. Don't let that lack of understanding get in the way of forgiving the behavior if you are able to do so.

▧ The listener will have three response choices to every forgiveness request at the end of each item:

  a. "Yes, I will forgive you."

  b. "No, I cannot forgive you."

  c. "Not now. I cannot forgive you now, but I am working on it."

▧ At the end of the reading, each second and third choice items (i.e., "no" and "not now" responses) should be reread. Sometimes a spouse can forgive a particular item more easily after hearing the reading of the entire list.

▧ When you have finished reading and received forgiveness, reach across and hug your spouse while saying, "Thank you for your forgiveness."

▧ Exchange forgiveness letters after the reading and do the following evaluation in private. After finishing the following evaluation, sit down with your spouse and discuss your responses, one at a time.

Evaluation

Take some time after the reading of the letters to individually respond to these following questions. You might even want to write out some of your answers to better share them with your spouse:

- How do I feel overall, having gone through this exercise in forgiveness?
- Were there other areas of confession I would have liked to have heard? Why are these important to me?
- Do I need to clarify how his/her behavior affected me?
- Were there items I could not forgive? What behavior from my spouse do I need to see before I can forgive? Is it a matter of some time going by?

Cautions

First, remember that forgiving does not mean that the hurtful behavior will never happen again. It does mean that the spouse is aware of how their behavior hurts you, and therefore will not intentionally repeat it for the purpose of hurting you. Should this behavior happen again (and it may), be quick to verbalize your awareness of it and offer forgiveness.

And when you realize you've repeated hurtful behavior, acknowledge that you have done so and ask forgiveness.

Change takes time. Most of us can tolerate hurtful behavior when we see that our spouse is working hard at changing the pattern.

Second, whatever additional items your spouse identifies in the review need to be included at the end of your letter, so complete your letter by acknowledging the ways your behavior affected your spouse and with a request for forgiveness. Most of us don't identify all of our hurtful behaviors the first time through. So don't take offense at this; just follow through taking care of it.

Third, your spouse only has to ask for forgiveness for a specific item twice. You need to tell your spouse when you're ready to forgive. Make it specific. Tackle one unforgiven item at a time. Neither of you should assume that it is taken care of when the process hasn't been completed by a verbal statement "I forgive you for . . ."

TWO VITAL INGREDIENTS

Respect

When love is injured, the healing process looks like this:

Forgive ⇨ Respect ⇨ Trust

To the degree you can forgive, you can rebuild respect. And to the degree you respect, you can rebuild trust. If you find you cannot respect your spouse, look at forgiveness/unforgiveness issues. If you are struggling in the area of trust, look at respect issues.

Respect is a difficult attitude to grasp, but when it is absent, it is readily apparent. And even when it's present, spouses usually do not verbalize it to each other.

Take a look at this next activity, appropriately entitled R-E-S-P-E-C-T. Be aware of how an absence of respect can make you susceptible to a close call.

RESPECT QUIZ

	RARELY	SOMETIMES	FREQUENTLY
Do I put down my spouse when we are with friends?	☐	☐	☐
Do I point out my spouse's shortcomings to family members?	☐	☐	☐
Do I tease my spouse in private to the point that it hurts their feelings?	☐	☐	☐
Do I rehearse my spouse's shortcomings in my mind?	☐	☐	☐
Do I allow other people to "pick" on my spouse when we are together?	☐	☐	☐
Do I tell my spouse about their strengths?	☐	☐	☐
Do I tell my spouse how grateful I am for their love and support?	☐	☐	☐
Do I encourage my spouse to pursue their dreams?	☐	☐	☐
Do I take for granted all that my spouse provides in our marriage?	☐	☐	☐
Do I feel like I have an inferior position on my spouse's "totem pole"?	☐	☐	☐
Do I discount my spouse's opinions, especially in front of others?	☐	☐	☐
Do I feel put down, picked on, or ignored by my spouse when we are out with friends?	☐	☐	☐
Do I feel taken for granted by my spouse?	☐	☐	☐
Do I feel like I am a "project" for my spouse?	☐	☐	☐
When I receive "help" from my spouse, do I feel like they are trying to show me up or teach me a better way to do a particular task?	☐	☐	☐
Do I feel treated like a child?	☐	☐	☐

157

Trust

Have you or your spouse had a close call? Repeated close calls injure trust. Recurrent close calls are due to those signals an unhappy spouse is sending to those around him. Recurrent close calls are a way for the unhappy spouse to get attention, receive nurturance, create jealousy, and alleviate insecurities.

The pattern of flirting can have one of several sources ranging from childhood insecurities to historical adolescent behavior to a marital void, but whatever the cause, it erodes trust. It is not innocent. It is not just a game. You are not acting as though you and the person with whom you're flirting are just friends. You are milking these interactions to meet your emotional needs. Thus, you are robbing your marriage and disrespecting your spouse.

On the other hand, to share a close call with your spouse for the purpose of receiving support, encouragement, and freedom from the attraction usually develops a deeper respect and trust between the two of you.

As I have said throughout the book, most of us have close calls. It's not uncommon when you find out about one to initially feel betrayed by your spouse and for hypervigilance to kick in: Who is my wife talking to on the phone? Will my husband see someone today when I'm not with him? Anxiety and a general uneasiness often follow. You will know that trust is being restored when your spouse (the one who had the close call) becomes the hypervigilant one and starts doing whatever is necessary to replenish the trust between the two of you. If the reversal of this responsibility does not take place between the two of you, trust is in limbo and still injured.

Trust versus Feeling Taken for Granted

As I have listened over the years as a counselor to husbands and wives who have had extramarital affairs, I have noticed the frequency of these types of statements: "I never thought . . ." or

"No one would believe that she..." or "He was such a perfect..."

Initially, I was impressed with the level of trust that these spouses appeared to have in their betrayers. Then I began to realize that they didn't *actively* trust their spouse — they just assumed that they would never be betrayed. Trust that has not been nurtured, stretched, and kept alive in a relationship feels like "being taken for granted." You know the difference. You know when you're being trusted or when you're being taken for granted. You feel grateful when you're being trusted. You feel unimportant when you're being taken for granted.

When you are trusted, you can talk about difficult subjects. When you are taken for granted, conversation has to be safe. You don't want to rock the boat, so you stay quiet. When you are trusted, your conversations are eye-to-eye. When you are taken for granted, you feel invisible. When you are taken for granted, your spouse is not interested in your likes and dislikes. They think they already know and have you figured out. You are not allowed to change. When you are trusted, both of you find these adjustments interesting fodder for conversation, and the changes are stimulating rather than threatening.

LEARNING TO TRUST

So how does one build this living, exhilarating, daily kind of trust? It is built and nurtured on four basic concepts:

- Structure (agreed-upon rules): "I know exactly what is going to happen."
- Safety (freedom from pain): "I can relax in the other person's presence."
- Nonsexual touch: "I won't be taken advantage of."
- Speech tone and content: "I can listen without fear of being demeaned."

An infant's first developmental stage is usually called "trust versus mistrust," and often it determines how trusting that child will become of his or her environment. It is an awareness that "I can relax; it is safe here" or "I have caregivers close by to protect me and who will look after my well-being" or "I don't have to be on my guard now."

This process also occurs in a serious dating relationship as couples draw closer to a lifelong commitment. Their interactions have grown increasingly more intimate and exclusive over time. They say things to each other and share secrets with each other that they do not share with anyone else. They are trusting each other. Trust grows to the conviction that "this is the one for me," and the couple eventually make some vows to seal their selection. You learn how to trust first in infancy without a choice of who you have to learn to trust, and you do it a second time when you make a mate selection. Sometimes in the case of close calls, especially with those that lead to adultery, you have to work through trust a third time. *All trust is built by the same process.*

When Trust Is Injured

If trust has been injured in a close call or by some other combination of painful experiences, the following four practices have to be consistently implemented over time in order to heal the injury:

- **No surprises.** This lowers the startle response and removes the hypervigilance that often accompanies near betrayal.

- **Informing prior to the fact.** Don't wait for your spouse to hear of last-minute changes. Take the initiative. Contact beforehand with changes.

- **Keep your word.** Go where you say you will go. Be where you say you will be. Make deadlines. Be responsible. Be on time.

- **Don't keep secrets.** Don't hide. Stop being defensive. Voice tone needs to be honest and upbeat, and content needs to be an open book.

In most cases a spouse wants to trust, so make it easy for them to do so.

Go through the discussion on the next page and talk honestly and openly with your spouse. Be an attentive listener.

A MATTER OF TRUST

Are there any surprise areas in our marriage that create a sense of "I wonder what's going to happen next"?	
Are there areas where I wait until the last minute to inform my spouse, hoping that things will work out for the best?	
What is my history and my spouse's history of "keeping my word"?	
Am I defensive? In what areas?	
Do I force my spouse to ask a perfect question to get the answer they are looking for?	
Where did I learn this pattern?	
What do I get out of this pattern?	
Why did I start practicing it?	
How does my spouse get "around" this?	

HALT-B

The acronym HALT has been around for decades in 12-step relapse prevention programs. It stands for:

H – Hungry

A – Angry

L – Lonely

T – Tired

I added the "B" when it quickly became apparent that many adulterers were BORED in their marriages. So what does this mean and how is it helpful?

Think of these five descriptions as mood states. The more of them that are present at any one point of time — an afternoon, an evening, a late night — the more likely one is to relapse. Or another way to view it, the more likely one is to break through whatever boundaries have been established for protection.

It is common knowledge in addiction recovery that these mood states often contributed to recovering alcoholics slipping or relapsing. They were usually instructed that when they began to feel any of these feelings they were to contact their sponsor and not try to go it alone. These were the triggers to drink. These are still the triggers that provoke vulnerability to a close call.

Some of you might be saying, "What does hunger have to do with this?" Food and sex are basic needs. Alcoholics always drink when hungry. This is that feeling of emptiness that causes some to eat emotionally, others to drink, still others to act out sexually.

Anger is a bit more understandable. When you are upset with your spouse, frustrated that change seems impossible, or if you are living in the face of rage every day, a close call or even an affair seems appealing. You are desperate for someone to understand, someone to care.

Loneliness can happen in a crowd, and there is no worse feeling of loneliness than the one that happens in a marriage that early on held so much promise. We marry to get connected.

Exhaustion, the more extreme form of tiredness, is often a factor in the stories of adultery. It is the "worn-out" feeling that comes from years of effort. It can also be the simple tiredness of burning the candle at both ends over a recent period of time. Whatever the source, you just don't have the power to resist the immediate temptation.

Finally, there is the boredom, that dullness that comes from too much predictability. Even the best of experiences can take on this flavor if there is no contrast. It is just more of the same, over and over.

I remind you that these are mood states, a frame of mind, a set of feelings, the more of which are present at a given time can easily erode the best boundaries. Pay attention to what is going on inside you. Know yourself. Don't be too proud to ask for help — don't try to go through life alone. Small groups, accountability partners (of your same sex), and church friends are all excellent resources as a sounding board when you need one — as we all do from time to time — and as encouragement to keep your marriage fresh.

COULD THIS BE YOU?

As you start to read this story, you will notice immediately all the changes that this couple had to make. They were both in agreement on their initial decision, but their one move turned into twenty-one moves in the next five years! After school, they never took the time to reorient themselves with each other. They never checked out each other's satisfaction with the relationship, and all those moves were followed by a steep decline in marital satisfaction and an escalation in conflict. Still, this couple could not stop themselves from doing what they both hated.

Here are Jaclyn's own words:

"Ten years ago Jimmy wanted to go back to school. In order for him to do that, we needed to live in a rural community, so that meant leaving the city that we lived in and leaving the church that we had attended for years. It was hard for me but I wanted to support my husband. To make a real long story short, we, with our four children, ended up moving twenty times in five years.

"When my husband got done with school and was offered a position, he promised me that I could have the house I wanted. I had lived in rentals and student housing and had never once in those five years completely unpacked our boxes. He knew how important it was for me to be settled and in the house that I wanted. That never came to pass because he had his own requirements. He wanted it to be in the country with acreage so he could have horses. We finally found a house that he absolutely had to have because of the acreage, but the house was falling down, and the whole inside needed to be gutted.

"When we moved into the house we spent every dime we had and every spare minute working on it. I hated it, and the kids hated it. I craved stability and family time, and my husband was growing bitter because we wouldn't help him work on the house. I confessed my frustration and sin of resentment to my husband many times and asked him to forgive me, which he always did. After about two years of this, Jimmy, as he says, "snapped," and his heart went cold, and he had no feelings for me or the kids.

"I saw him slipping away from us and many times would

tell him we should go to counseling or something. I would scream at him to please be my friend. Little did I know that nine months before this time he had found someone else to be his friend. It was not a relationship that he enjoyed being in except for the emotional friendship that he had with her. She didn't nag him, he had no responsibility for her, and it was relaxing.

"I see my contribution in the deterioration of our marriage because I nagged him to be a dad (I thought I was advocating for the kids), to stop working on the house (the house, in fact, is still not done, and we've been working on it for five years), to be a husband, and I would often mention how I hated the house and how he didn't live up to his promise to let me have the house that I wanted."

NOTE

1. An excellent resource on the whole issue of apology and forgiveness is *The Five Languages of Apology* by Gary Chapman and Jennifer Thomas.

BARRIERS TO CLOSE CALLS

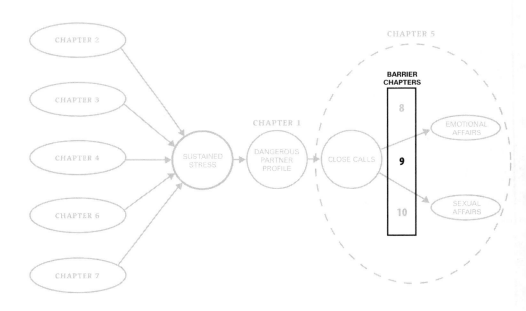

9 ACTIVITIES:

Reignite Infatuation

Max and Alison were comfortable. Their weekly routine included work for Max, part-time work and busyness with the kids for Alison, chores on Saturday, church on Sunday morning, and watching sports on Sunday afternoon. An occasional outing to a movie or a "Let's order a pizza for supper" was about the extent of shaking up their everyday lives. They were happy, though ... at least they thought they were happy enough.

But when Alison was appointed to the Sunday school picnic committee with Darren, suddenly there was a heightened interest in the most daily of chores: counting up how many hot dog buns would be needed, figuring out the amount of ketchup and relish needed, going out shopping together. Alison and Darren were a good team, and Alison unexpectedly found herself having something new to look forward to; she felt that she was waking up after a long sleep. She made up reasons to phone him, suggested extra meetings, set aside items for conversation.

Around this time, Max was sent on a two-day business trip with Brenda, a coworker he'd been acquainted with for over a year. They sat together on the plane and got to know each other for the first time beyond work. Max was enjoying the conversation, and realized it was the first time in a long time that his stories were amusing to this attractive woman, stories that Alison had long ago grown bored with. Max arranged for the two of them to have dinner together "to prepare for the presentation tomorrow." To his surprise, he noticed that he was taking far more care to look good for her than he did for Alison and was planning how he could spend more time with Brenda when the trip was over.

You know by now where both Alison and Max are headed, don't you? Close call!

Many people who have a close call — or a close call that leads to an affair — are looking for the excitement that has faded from their marriage. Their marriages and daily lives had become routine, predictable, and boring.

So how does a couple begin to redevelop these special kinds of experiences? Well, one key is thinking back on how the two of you started your relationship. For most couples that meant cheap dates. It meant finding ways to have fun even when you didn't have that much money.

So the next exercise you're going to do will help you identify some of those experiences, as well as others in the marriage that are highlights in your relationship. These are the grand events that convinced you that you were made for each other. They don't have to be dramatic dates, just great memories. You cannot list anything that has to do with your children, other couples, or your wedding day (the honeymoon, however, is an option).

RECREATING GREAT MOMENTS AND MAKING THEM NEW

Eight Greats

Each of you is to list what you consider to be the top eight great experiences in your relationship. You will notice that there are three columns on next page: the experience, the season of the year, and the location. Some of your experiences will undoubtedly be influenced by where you were at the time and the season of the year in which you had this experience, so those are important components.

After you have written out the eight greats for yourself, sit back and take a look at these highlights. How do you feel looking at this list? How long has it been since you had an "eight great" experience? It's not too late to recapture the feeling, so the next step is to merge your two lists. After you have written down the matching items, the wife chooses the next one, the husband chooses the next, and so forth, until you have your merged list. The excitement these kinds of experiences generates is often the kinds of things people will look for outside their marriage if they don't find them with their spouse.

Get started adding excitement back to your relationship with your mate! Redo what you do best! It doesn't matter what it costs; enhancing and protecting your marriage is worth it!

This can even be sort of a restoration project for an older marriage. By "redoing" I mean going back to the exact place, in the same season of the year, and experience the original great moment. No shortcuts allowed—that only cheapens the final product. If the memory took place when you were exchange students in Europe, then go back to Europe! If there was a college football game, go back to the same stadium, same game, and same seats, if possible. Rehearse what made this memory great. Anyone in the restoration business will tell you that the process is expensive, but just like value is added to an old car or an historic building when it is rebuilt to its original specifications, so,

EIGHT GREAT MOMENTS

EXPERIENCE	SEASON OF THE YEAR	LOCATION
Personal List		
1.		
2.		
3.		
4.		
5.		
6.		
7.		
8.		
Merged List		
1.		
2.		
3.		
4.		
5.		
6.		
7.		
8.		

too, will you both be restored when you rebuild your marriage on your original great experiences.

Rituals

A close call relationship quickly develops rituals. Rituals have nothing to do with the calendar, but rather they are the regular, anticipated experiences that create little disappointments if they don't happen. Men and women who have committed adultery talk about the rituals they established with their partner: their phone call times, their meeting places, their coffee shops.

Dating couples have rituals, but most marriages don't. Rituals are often set aside for expedience — hectic schedules, finances, schooling, lack of energy. A ritual is something that just the two of you are involved in. While being with family members or your children or other couples can be wonderful experiences, they do not count as building "your history." Take a look at the questions below, and spend some time reflecting on the rituals you might have once shared, those you share now, and still others that you need to build into your relationship.

- What rituals did we practice while dating?
- What rituals did we have prior to children?
- What rituals have we abandoned ("Remember when we used to ... ?")
- What rituals do we currently practice?
- What rituals do we need to develop?

What do you think of your list? What do you think your spouse will think? This is a fun talk, so don't make it heavy and hurtful.

Compliment Prayer List

I learned about the protective nature of this final exercise by listening to adulterers tell me how they lost sight of what they once thought was so great about their spouse when they were involved with the partner. It is an exercise that calms anxiety, diminishes feelings of insecurity, provides reassurance, and lowers hypervigilance. It will fuel chemistry between you and your spouse and add the kind of excitement some people might misguidedly look outside the marriage for.

People who get involved in affairs do not focus on, rehearse, review, or remind their partner of their weaknesses! They are intensely centered on the things they like about each other. That is why they are so infatuated with each other. Now I know that becomes unrealistic when living with someone 24/7. And in a marriage in which this kind of verbal affirmation hasn't been practiced much ("We never did this much in my family, and I don't need it"), it can be a bit uncomfortable to start. So here is a way to say these things in front of your spouse but to someone else — God! — in a prayer. Here are the instructions:

- You each have your own assignment notebook.
- You use one page per day.
- You identify a new compliment every day, one day at a time.
- You do this for thirty straight days.
- You pray out loud in each other's presence.

The compliment can be a behavior, belief, skill, a look, a response; anything that you like or admire in your spouse. You write the new compliment at the top of a new page followed by two or three sentences elaborating on how and why you like this trait. Together you utter your prayer at the agreed-upon time. "Dear God, thank You for _____ that I see in (name). I love it when I experience it when _____." Your spouse prays a similar prayer.

At the end of thirty days, you exchange notebooks. You now have a list of what your spouse likes best about you. Look at it often, and do the exercise on a regular basis, even without the little notebook. You can't repeat an item, and you don't list several of the same type of things, e.g., her lasagna, her fried chicken. In this case, you would list her effort at cooking meals you enjoy.

When my wife and I first tried this exercise, one of my choices was my wife's great smile. I told her how much I loved to see her smile at me. Then I listed the ways and times I liked it the best: when I entered a room and first caught her eye, when I first walked in the house in the evening, and when we had had a disagreement and had worked through it. You get the picture — now get started. Most spouses are desperate to hear this kind of recognition.

THAT SEXUAL PIZZAZZ

When a couple hops into bed on their wedding night, they will find six people sleeping there: her mom and dad, his mom and dad, and the two of them! The bad news? It will take you several years to clarify what the two of you are going to practice in your sexual relationship compared to what you learned and saw practiced in each of your families of origin. When a close call or even infidelity occurs in a marriage of seven years or less, there is almost always some influence from family of origin issues involved.

Sexual History

Even virgins have a well-developed sexual history. Is this a startling statement? It shouldn't be. The brain is still the most dominant sexual organ, and good sex is still very much about good attitudes. What has been modeled to us is the most powerful determinant on our behavior there is. Teens might act disgusted when talking about their parents' sexual relationship, but they are intuitively aware of how each parent views that part of the relationship in the marriage.

So what did you pick up at home that you brought with you into your marriage? To help you sort through some of that, consider the statements below. I've used them as a survey for premarital classes for over two decades. The purpose is to help couples clarify their attitudes about sex, to become aware of how they have been influenced both positively and negatively about sex, to realize what they need to let go of (". . . leave your mother and father"), and to give them permission to talk about what can be a difficult subject for many couples. If you feel uncertain about your memory of some of your perceptions, consider talking with your siblings.

Even if you've been married for many years, this survey will help you clarify what you still might believe about marital sex even though you left your family of origin long ago. Attitudes about sexuality have longevity; they are often so ingrained in our nature that they are difficult to identify and root out. This is a time when you both might feel vulnerable, so listen and learn from each other.

As with other activities throughout the book, first look at all of your answers before sharing them with your spouse. It might be easier to write the answers.

- Three words my dad would have used to describe the sexual relationship with my mom in their marriage are:
- Three words my mom would have used to describe the sexual relationship with my dad in their marriage are:
- I would describe my impressions about sexuality growing up this way:
- I would describe my impressions about sexuality in adolescence this way:

▨ Our family attitude toward sexuality was:

▨ Sex was used in my parents' marriage as/to:

▨ Three words I would use to describe our sex life are:

▨ My greatest fear about sex is:

▨ Sex to my spouse means:

What is the overall impression that your answers give you about your sexual attitudes? Surprised?

Do you think your spouse will be surprised by your responses?

What differences can you identify between your sexual attitudes and those of each of your parents?

Would you like for your children to model the attitudes you see by your responses? If not, why? What changes do you need to make?

Do you think your sexual attitudes are in line with the spiritual beliefs you acknowledge in your life?

Make some notes on these questions and plan a time to talk with your spouse about these issues.

Nonsexual Touch

I always smile at the response of some people to the phrase "nonsexual touch." Some individuals respond immediately by saying, "I am not the touchy-feely type." That's not true! It never was true!

The fact is that we are all desperate for touch. It's a part of the soothing process that God built into the parasympathetic nervous system. It provides the calming effect on a distraught child that is well-known to every parent. Every dating couple is crazy about getting their hands on each other. The need to touch has been built into the attraction.

What has happened to many couples is that they have restricted touch to eroticism and a signal for sex. Unfortunately, touch that always leads to sexual activity almost always curtails touching activity. So touching and caressing, those great nurturing experiences, disappear from many relationships. These couples settle for less than either spouse really wants.

The opposite should be true. It was when you started dating. Consider this—close calls always have incidental touch in their initial stages. Nothing overt and nothing sexual, just a light caress that sends chills up the spine of the one who receives it. Don't tell me you are not touchy-feely!

So touch is one of the primary ways couples build trust initially between the two of them. Almost every marriage needs more of these experiences, so as you began to practice them, make sure you stay within the following boundaries:

- Each of these activities is twenty minutes in length.
- Never let these activities lead directly to erotic touching or sexual activity.
- The receiver chooses the type of touching exercise he or she wants.
- Take turns being the giver and receiver.
- It is okay for the receiver to fall asleep during the exercise.
- The giver should be looking at the body part they are stroking.
- The caress needs to be slow, with single finger contact on the receiver's skin.

Sometimes couples are resistant to doing these exercises for several reasons:

- ▨ They are afraid of being misinterpreted or manipulated by their spouse.

- ▨ The marriage has never had much nonsexual touch, and it feels uncomfortable to start now.

- ▨ One spouse is currently angry with the other.

- ▨ One spouse feels sexually aroused and views this exercise as a waste of time (this is a very common response in cases where couples have conditioned themselves over time to use touch as a signal for sex).

- ▨ There is a history of abusive touch.

NON-SEXUAL TOUCHING EXERCISES [1]

Purpose: To nurture, rebuild trust, and to reinforce boundaries

	HAND	FOOT	HEAD
SETTING	Seated beside each other, arm resting comfortably in giver's lap	Giver seated on a couch with legs of receiver resting on lap	Giver seated on a couch with head of receiver resting on lap
BOUNDARY	The elbow	The knee	The shoulders
PRACTICE	Light, slow predictable	Massage with lotion	Light, slow, and exploratory
TIME	5 minutes on each side of hand and forearm, total 20 minutes	10 minutes per leg and foot	5 minutes right side of head; 10 minutes face; 5 minutes left side of head

Source: Adapted from Cliff and Joyce Penner, *The Gift of Sex* (Waco, TX:Word, 1981), 141–45.

SCRIPT LINES CHECKLIST

Check the lines that apply to experiences you have had and that you have said or could imagine saying.

☐ 1. I feel uncomfortable.

☐ 2. I think your stroking feels mechanical.

☐ 3. I feel I'm supposed to like everything you are doing.

☐ 4. I am worried about what you're thinking.

☐ 5. That doesn't feel good but I know what would.

☐ 6. It feels like you're being too careful.

☐ 7. It feels like you're trying too hard.

☐ 8. I resent that you're enjoying this more.

☐ 9. I don't know why we're doing this.

☐ 10. I wish it was OK to ignore you.

☐ 11. I feel hopeless about ever turning you on.

☐ 12. Right now my mind is blank.

☐ 13. I wish I felt more like stroking you.

☐ 14. I wish I could enjoy your stroking.

☐ 15. This is a chore for me.

☐ 16. I'm not feeling anything.

☐ 17. I don't feel like talking.

☐ 18. I feel a million miles away.

☐ 19. This seems difficult and complicated.

☐ 20. I feel turned off.

☐ 21. I'm afraid you're going to feel rejected if I don't enjoy this more.

☐ 22. I feel like you need me to be more involved.

☐ 23. I want something, but I don't know what it is.

☐ 24. I don't think I'm going to like anything we're doing today.

☐ 25. I think I'm mostly doing this because I'm supposed to.

SCRIPT LINES CHECK LIST (continued)

☐ 26. I'm beginning to be impatient.

☐ 27. You seem preoccupied (or far away).

☐ 28. I feel like there's something else I want to say, but it's not in any of these scripts.

☐ 29. I'm afraid I'm not going to do a good enough job.

☐ 30. I'm afraid you're going to be disappointed.

☐ 31. I'm getting distracted.

☐ 32. I wish we could play hookey from this.

☐ 33. My mind keeps going off into fantasies.

☐ 34. I feel obliged to do as much for you as you have done for me.

☐ 35. I'm afraid you are getting bored.

☐ 36. I'm afraid you won't tell me if you don't like something.

☐ 37. I feel like we both have to succeed at this.

☐ 38. I'm feeling lazy but like I'm not allowed to.

☐ 39. I'm feeling that there's too much I don't like.

☐ 40. I'm afraid of discouraging you.

☐ 41. I'm feeling too finicky.

☐ 42. I'd feel like a pest if I said everything I wanted.

☐ 43. I'd like to take a break.

☐ 44. I'm afraid you'd get mad if I stopped doing this.

☐ 45. I wish this wasn't so important.

☐ 46. I feel like there's something you want, but I don't know what it is.

☐ 47. I feel like I should appreciate what you are doing more.

☐ 48. It feels like something just went wrong, but I don't know what it is.

☐ 49. I can't seem to concentrate on what I'm doing.

☐ 50. I hate these script lines.

Source: Bernard Apfelbaum, "Ego Analytic Perspective on Desire Disorders," in *Sexual Desire Disorders*, ed. Sandra R. Leiblum and Raymond C. Rosen (New York: Guilford, 1992).

Going through the script lines checklist on pages 180–181 is one of the best ways to handle resistance to this exercise. It was developed by the Berkeley Sex Therapy Group and is used with permission.[2] It contains fifty negative statements about being touched, and in most cases will capture the thoughts going through your mind while considering or even doing this set of exercises. Even if you as a couple are looking forward to doing these exercises, it would still be a good idea to look through the list sometime after doing the touching exercise. Most of these statements have a history; i.e., this is not the first time that you felt this way about giving or receiving touch. That history can make for some very interesting and informative discussions between you and your spouse, another step toward building deeper intimacy.

COULD THIS BE YOU?

This account is very straightforward. Though there are many risk factors mentioned in this note, Susan does not use them as an excuse. Instead she acknowledges both her contributions to the marital deterioration and her husband's unmet needs satisfied in the other woman — the respect he needs and deserves. Susan's journey to this new level of awareness is one that every spouse needs to go through after a close call. Instead of despair and guilt that many suppose results from such a journey, you can see that just the opposite is true — it produces hope. At the end of her e-mail, Susan expresses a profound confidence that she and Casey can make it. I hope they did!

Susan says:

"He has not made his final decision as to whether or not he wants to come home again. He is having trouble believing that our marriage could survive this or even be better because of it.

"Our marriage had about ten years of turmoil during the time of raising babies, financial difficulties, death of all our parents, working different shifts, and my lack of trying. I wasn't very nice to Casey during much of it, and he wasn't there for me either. I suppose that I fell into the mind-set that I deserved more out of life.

"However, during the year prior to our splitting I really saw that everything I thought I was searching for in life was right here in my husband and family all along. By then it was too late. Casey had found someone else who wanted to be with him and who treated him with the respect he deserved. He became angry with the way our lives had been going and felt justified in moving out. He chose to get involved with a married woman, the neighbor's wife. It seemed so easy for him to leave me and our kids. She left her second husband, and moved with her kids into a house with Casey. They have been together there for one year.

"After this year of fighting, begging, crying, pleading, praying, and soul-searching, we have come to realize how we both contributed to the demise of our marriage, but neither of us is settled in our lives apart. Although he says he's 'in love' with her, he says he also still loves me. He has never filed for divorce, and can't imagine calling me his 'Ex.'

"I made the mistake of trying these last few months to go out on dates, thinking it would help me move on. But Casey is my main focus, and I feel like we haven't given ourselves a chance to reconcile and work on our marriage. I cannot seem to let go.

"I truly do love him, and want to make our marriage work. For me there is way more than 20 percent of our marriage I would rate as a 4–5. I believe that I can work through this with him and forgive him. I have contributed enough that there can be no judgment. He seems to think that I will win him back and then leave him as vindication for this painful period.

"I believe that with God, nothing is impossible. I believe that Casey and I together, with God's help, can accomplish ANYTHING. I believe that there is forgiveness and healing even after something like this. I believe we can have a wonderful marriage and family, now that we have started communicating."

NOTES

1. This exercise was adapted from Cliff and Joyce Penner, *The Gift of Sex* (Waco, TX: Word, 1981), 141–45.

2. Bernard Apfelbaum, "Ego Analytic Perspective on Desire Disorders," in *Sexual Desire Disorders*, ed. Sandra R. Leiblum and Raymond C. Rosen (New York: Guilford, 1992). Script lines also appeared in Dave Carder, *Torn Asunder Workbook* (Chicago: Moody, 2001), 81–82.

BARRIERS TO CLOSE CALLS

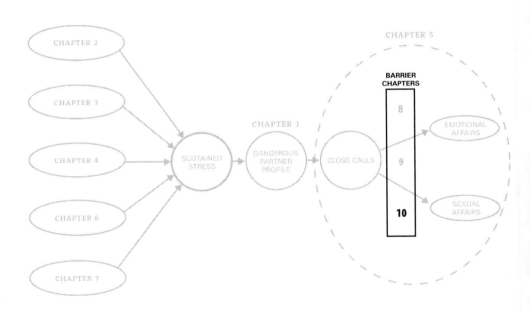

10 AWARENESS:
Environmental Practices

Well, we've covered a lot of material. You might be a bit overwhelmed, especially if you went through the book in a random fashion. So in this final chapter, I am going to lay out a review of the content. Each chapter review will have a theme to help you understand how it all fits together. There will be a Close Call Contract for you and your spouse to read through and sign. I will share with you a list of simple dos and don'ts to protect your marriage in this close call culture. Finally, I will provide you with a Friendship Quiz that will help both of you assess your friendships with the opposite sex.

Many times a spouse is unaware of how deeply involved they are in a friendship or how often they even mention his or her friend's name in conversations until after they have taken this evaluation. Here is a nice way to lay out some concrete information on how you feel about your spouse's friend. It will keep the blaming to a minimum and the emotions out of the discussion.

Chapter 1:

RISKY ATTRACTIONS: *Do You Know One?*

Reminder: Stay away from anyone who fits your dangerous partner profile!

Not all men or women are equally attractive to you. There is, however, a profile composite of all of your life experiences that makes a member of the opposite sex especially appealing to you. Intuitively, most of us choose a spouse who is very different from this personal temptation.

Chapter 2:

RISKY FACTORS: *What Are Yours?*

Reminder: Stay aware of your high-risk factors.

Research has identified risk factors from your family of origin as well as personal factors. Know your story, because what you bring *to* the marriage is going have an impact on your choices *in* marriage.

Chapter 3:

RISKY HISTORY: *Do You Have One?*

Reminder: Be aware of your high-risk season of life.

Our lives and our marriages go through seasons. Recognize how times of loss, transition, and your own behavior can bring on risks of close calls.

Chapter 4:

RISKY MARRIAGE: *Are You in One?*

Reminder: Get a handle on your history and when the most satisfying times have been.

All marriages go through seasons or stages of experience, and certain seasons are more vulnerable to infidelity. Your Marital Satisfaction Time Line will help the two of you make better sense of your history, as well as plan certain improvements in your relationship.

Chapter 5:

CLOSE CALLS *and the Affairs They Can Lead To*

Reminder: Learn about the characteristics of close calls, as well as the four classes of extramarital affairs.

Chapter 6:

THE CLOSE CALL MARRIAGE: *Your Marital Style*

Reminder: Stay focused on marital flexibility

Marriages can get locked into patterns, even good patterns that over time can create boredom within the relationship. Three of these common patterns, identified by research as especially susceptible to adultery, are reviewed. One of them might match yours.

Chapter 7:

THE CLOSE CALL VACUUM: *Your Marital Dance*

Reminder: You may have borrowed your patterns of interaction from your family of origin without even realizing it.

Chapter 8:

ATTITUDES: *Exterior and Interior*

Reminder: Trust, respect, and a determination to eliminate boredom are excellent preventatives to having close calls.

Chapter 9:

ACTIVITIES: *Reignite Infatuation*

Reminder: Stay committed to doing what you used to do best — being vulnerable and having fun.

Affair-free, long-lasting marriages have a history of creating multiple mini-affairs with each other across the time they've been together. You don't need to go outside your marriage to have fun if the two of you will return to doing what you used to do best. Identify your Eight Greats and get started.

Well, that's where we have been, but here is a final word from my friends who slipped from close calls into having adulterous affairs. Don't discount what they say — remember, not paying attention to these are how most adulterers got involved in close calls that led to devastating extramarital affairs. And in my years as a postadultery recovery counselor, I've never met an adulterer who didn't regret what he or she had done.

Here are what adulterers want you to know about protecting your marriage:

The Don'ts and Dos of Living in a Close Call Culture

With members of the opposite sex:

- Don't do lunch alone.
- Don't talk about personal issues.
- Don't listen to talk about personal issues.
- Don't meet outside required work hours.
- Don't think you can handle temptation by yourself; find a friend with whom to be accountable.
- Do acknowledge and be aware of your high-risk factors.
- Do know your HALT-B state of being.
- Do stay away from your dangerous partner.
- Do spend money on your marriage.
- Do go to sleep with your spouse together (staying up late by yourself is a recipe for temptation).

Friendships with Members of the Opposite Sex

As you've read, thought through, and discussed the concepts in this book, you might have thought about a relationship you have with someone of the opposite sex. These relationships are seductive and very easily begin to mean too much to both parties. It is a simple step, easily made, to start saving conversational topics for the friendship, thus robbing the marriage of emotional nurturance.

Here is an evaluation to help the two of you take stock of just how close these opposite-sex friendships might be to each of you. As always, listen to each other. Don't blame each other; it happens very easily to all us.

FRIENDSHIP QUIZ

		YES	NO
1.	Do you save topics of conversation for your friend because you feel they understand you better?	☐	☐
2.	Have you shared spousal difficulties with this friend under the guise of wanting to understand your spouse better?	☐	☐
3.	Has your friend shared difficulties they are having with relationships?	☐	☐
4.	Do you find yourself looking forward to seeing your friend more than you look forward to seeing your spouse?	☐	☐
5.	Do you find yourself comparing your spouse to this friend?	☐	☐
6.	Are you providing special and thoughtful treats, cards, for your friend?	☐	☐
7.	Are you checking on your friend's welfare more frequently and with more concern than you check on the welfare of your spouse?	☐	☐
8.	Have you ever fantasized about what it would be like to be married to this friend?	☐	☐
9.	Are you spending more focused alone time with your friend than you spend similar time with your spouse?	☐	☐
10.	Are you comfortable letting your spouse review all of your telephone interactions, e-mail, text messages, and voice mails?	☐	☐
11.	Are you spending money on your friendship for lunches, gifts, coffee, that your spouse is unaware of?	☐	☐
12.	Are you and your spouse in conflict over this friendship?	☐	☐
13.	Do you find yourself lying or manipulating the truth in order to spend more time with this friend?	☐	☐
14.	Are you hiding receipts, cell phone bills, mail, gifts, and time spent with your friend from your spouse?	☐	☐

FRIENDSHIP QUIZ

		YES	NO
15.	Have you ever gotten angry or accused your spouse of jealousy when the topic of this friendship has been brought up between the two of you?	☐	☐
16.	Have you developed specific rituals, practices, and places with your friend?	☐	☐
17.	Has your friend shared feelings for you or touched you in a way that created a shiver of infatuation in you?	☐	☐
18.	Has any of the conversations with your friend had sexual or erotic content in them?	☐	☐
19.	Do you do any of the following with this friend:		
	a. travel	☐	☐
	b. go to entertainment venues	☐	☐
	c. drink alcohol	☐	☐
	d. eat expensive meals	☐	☐
	e. return to the same hotel	☐	☐

Close Call Contract

As I have said throughout this book, close calls will happen. But the most powerful way to disarm them is to talk to your spouse about the experience. Following is a contract that the two of you can use to develop this practice. It will guarantee a whole new level of intimacy between the two of you. It will help you create safety, keep respect high, nourish your trust, and make you feel important to your spouse. It will help provide what you as a couple want in marriage. Read it, adjust it if you need to, but sign it — then practice it!

OUR CLOSE CALL CONTRACT

We hereby acknowledge that:

- We live in a *Close Call Culture*

- It is normal to feel attracted to members of the opposite sex

- These attractions can be secretly cultivated and developed if we don't share them with each other

As a result, I promise to:

- tell you when I feel attracted to a particular individual

- listen to you if you feel someone is attracted to me

- listen to you with respect when you share an attraction

I further promise:

- not to react angrily to this information

- to discuss openly and honestly with you about this attraction

- to work enthusiastically with you to adjust our relationship to better meet our identified needs

- to never knowingly cultivate a friendship with someone of the opposite sex

Sign and date:

_____	_____	_____
HUSBAND	DATE	WIFE

We are done! Now we've concluded our time with the contract that the two of you have signed to enhance your present and protect your future. It is a step beyond your verbal commitments that you made in front of an audience on your wedding day. So stay strong. Stay close. Keep talking.

And fully enjoy the time that God is giving you together!

COULD THIS BE YOU?

I have saved the best for last. Though the story doesn't focus on the development of the close call, it does relay, in great detail, the pain that a close call, followed by an affair, generates in the marriage. It also demonstrates what the adulterer needs to do to help the marriage recover. If you are reading this book and your close call relationship has stepped across the boundary into the sexual arena, there is still hope for you. It won't be easy. That opportunity ended when you refused to leave the close call. But you still can recover, and, in most cases, you can still make your marriage good — or even better. Just follow the pattern you read in the e-mail from Angela below:

"Three months ago, I discovered my husband had had an affair. My world was shattered and my heart was broken. I couldn't imagine our marriage surviving this; I immediately asked my husband to leave our home. We are both Christians, but I could not fathom how even God could repair this kind of brokenness, nor was I sure I wanted to ask Him to.

"Long story short, my husband did not leave. He was truly repentant and asked for forgiveness. Before he disclosed the affair, he had prayed for the restoration of our marriage. He said God revealed that He could heal our marriage, but my husband first had to 'come out of the cover of darkness and into the light with the truth.'

"I knew by his changed spirit that God was working on

him, but I was initially too angry and too devastated to even speak to him. I desperately searched for spiritual guidance, and I saw your book *Torn Asunder* recommended on the Focus on the Family Web site. I ordered it and began reading it the moment it arrived. I began to look at my situation through spiritual eyes for the first time, and I felt God calming and comforting me.

"I told my husband about the book, and he began reading it. He soaked in every word on every page. He could not put the book down. He wanted to talk about everything he had learned from the book and the parallels with our situation. It helped to reopen the doors of communication between us. We talked for hours upon hours, and we continue to do so.

"My husband stayed in our home, and in retrospect I am so glad he did. As you said in your book, the infidel spouse needs to see and feel the pain he caused. My husband let me scream, shout, cry, and say anything I wanted to. He sat on the floor at my feet for hours as I wept uncontrollably . . . sometimes all through the night. He wept silently as I let it all out . . . over and over and over. He never blamed me; he allowed me to voice everything and anything I was feeling. He gave me space when I needed it. He took full responsibility for what he had done and kept telling me it was in no way my fault. It was his mistake, his sin, and he prayed I would choose to forgive him and try to survive this terrible crisis.

"He knew God had already forgiven him, but he did not know if I could. He said he would understand if I wanted to end our marriage over this, and he could not blame me if I made that choice, but he wanted more than anything for us to stay together and work it out. He committed to being totally transparent as you recommended in your book, and he has been true to that commitment. He also was struck very hard by your comments on how infidelity can run in families, so to speak.

"He cried a lot over that realization as he reflected on his upbringing and that of his children (by his first marriage). He bought two more copies of *Torn Asunder*, drove to another state to see his two adult children, and he admitted his affair to them. He allowed them to see his brokenness, which was a very bold thing for him to do. He discussed what he had learned through your book, and he gave each of his children a copy and asked them to read it. They talked for hours together. He came home and said, 'It was the hardest thing I've ever had to do with my kids, but I believe God directed me to have this talk with them. If my discussion with them about this can prevent them from causing the pain I have caused you, or can prevent them from feeling the pain I have caused us both, then it was worth the pain and embarrassment of admitting to them what I had done.'

"I have forgiven my husband. We have a long tough road ahead of us, and we are committed to working through it together. We are seeing a Christian counselor as well. The healing process is under way; God has already poured His blessings upon us in ways we cannot believe. We sought Him in our brokenness, and He is blessing us with His amazing grace, His comfort, His strength, and His encouragement in untold ways. We have come to see how we both stopped nurturing our relationship and let it go, and we never want to let that happen again. We feel like we have fallen in love with each other all over again . . . it's truly amazing."

APPENDIX

We've talked a lot throughout the book about sitting down with your wife or husband and going through the material on the charts and in the text. To have the most productive experiences doing this, make use of these descriptive words and also of the ideas on communication and conflict resolution. You can put these principles into practice in many future discussions and in many areas of life!

FEELING WORDS

MAD	SAD	GLAD	AFRAID
A LITTLE	A LITTLE	A LITTLE	A LITTLE
Bothered	Down	At Ease	Uneasy
Ruffled	Blue	Secure	Apprehensive
Irritated	Somber	Comfortable	Careful
Displeased	Low	Relaxed	Cautious
Annoyed	Glum	Contented	Hesitant
Steamed	Lonely	Optimistic	Tense
Irked	Disappointed	Satisfied	Anxious
Perturbed	Worn Out	Refreshed	Nervous
Frustrated	Melancholy	Stimulated	Edgy
Angry	Downhearted	Pleased	Distressed
Fed Up	Unhappy	Warm	Scared
Disgusted	Dissatisfied	Snug	Frightened
Indignant	Gloomy	Happy	Repulsed
Ticked Off	Mournful	Encouraged	Agitated
Bristling	Grieved	Tickled	Afraid
Fuming	Depressed	Proud	Shocked
Explosive	Lousy	Cheerful	Alarmed
Enraged	Crushed	Thrilled	Overwhelmed
Irate	Defeated	Delighted	Frantic
Incensed	Dejected	Joyful	Panic Stricken
Burned	Empty	Elated	Horrified
Burned Up	Wretched	Exhilarated	Petrified
Outraged	Despairing	Overjoyed	Terrified
Furious A LOT	Devastated A LOT	Ecstatic A LOT	Numb

CONFUSED	ASHAMED	LONELY
A LITTLE	A LITTLE	A LITTLE
Curious	Uncomfortable	Out of Place
Uncertain	Awkward	Left Out
Ambivalent	Clumsy	Unheeded
Doubtful	Self-Conscious	Lonesome
Unsettled	Disconcerted	Disconnected
Hesitant	Chagrined	Remote
Perplexed	Abashed	Invisible
Puzzled	Embarrassed	Unwelcome
Muddled	Flustered	Cut off
Distracted	Sorry	Excluded
Flustered	Apologetic	Insignificant
Jumbled	Ashamed	Ignored
Unfocused	Regretful	Neglected
Fragmented	Remorseful	Separated
Dismayed	Guilty	Removed
Insecure	Disgusted	Detached
Dazed	Belittled	Isolated
Bewildered	Humiliated	Unwanted
Lost	Violated	Rejected
Stunned	Dirty	Deserted
Chaotic	Mortified	Outcast
Torn	Defiled	Abandoned
Baffled	Devastated	Desolate
Dumbfounded A LOT	Degraded A LOT	Forsaken A LOT

Source: Beverly Hartz, "Pastoral Care and Chaplaincy" class notes, Fall 2000, Talbot Theological Seminary.

COMMUNICATION & CONFLICT RESOLUTION

How to Get Your Point Across Without Puncturing Someone in the Process

I. **OUTCOME:** A sense of being understood, cared for, accepted

II. **GOALS:**

TALKER (Teacher)
- Cannot use "you"
- Be specific and brief

LISTENER (Learner)
- Repress your own feeling and observations
- Summarize with same emotional intensity
- Summarize accurately even if you disagree

III. **PROCESS:** For Each Question (A–D)

A. Listener asks question
B. Talker responds
C. Listener summarizes
D. Talker approves or corrects
E. Listener summarizes
F. Listener asks next question

IV. **QUESTIONS:** (Always Asked by Listener)

A. "How do you see (view, etc.) this issue (problem, topic, etc.)?"

B. "When this happens, how does it make you feel?"
   Li   stener: Look for hurt, anger, or fear

C. "Can you tell me why you feel this way?"

D. "What do you need from me when you feel like that?"
   Listener: Listen for specific behaviors
   Talker: Slow down, think through what you need from listener
   when this issue arises. Make it a specific behavior

V. **CHANGE ROLES:** Go through the four basic questions (A-D) again.

   Talker: "How do you feel about what I just said?"
   (This is equivalent to question B)

VI. **TROUBLESHOOTING:**

A. If you as talker are feeling "attacked," the listener has assumed your role and is no longer listening.

B. If you as talker are feeling "grilled" or "interrogated," summaries are not being given often enough or at all.

C. If you as a listener are feeling "confused," not enough "feeling" words are being used.

D. Watch out for the talker who says "I feel . . ." but is using cognitions; if you can substitute "I think," then it is probably not a feeling.

E. If you as a listener are feeling "overwhelmed," slow conversation down; go "down" deeper into the topic instead of "across" it; limit feelings to those occurring in one issue at a time.

RESOURCES

INTERNET

www.eHarmony Marriage.com

Based on an in-depth marriage questionnaire and their personalized Marriage Profile, each couple is provided video exercises, direction, and tools that will improve their relationship. There is a lot of good information about your relationship strengths and style to put into practice.

www.marriagebuilders.com

Great articles on marriage and infidelity, but the real action is on the bulletin boards. Navigate to the "discussion forums" and you will find all the options. Language and anger are kept in check by a monitor. Good source for support and lots of good materials.

www.ocmarriage.org

Home page is called the Orange County Marriage Resource Center; it lists all the resources being provided in that county in that calendar month. Options change monthly. Resources are further broken down into five different marriage categories, plus there are other articles and suggestions for new parents, divorcing couples, and much more. Though the Web site lists only local offerings, most of these resources are available nationally and even internationally. This Web site is the brainchild of Dennis Stoica, who is committed to lowering the divorce rate in Orange County, California, by half in the next decade.

www.DearPeggy.com

A great site for articles, consultation, therapist lists, support for issues surrounding close calls. This crusader (Peggy Vaughan) has been involved in the marriage protection effort for almost thirty years.

www.preventingaffairs.com.

Peggy Vaughan's new book, *Preventing Affairs*, will soon be available through her site. If this book is anything like Peggy's other works (also see DearPeggy.com), it will be the front-runner very quickly with lots of research-based protections.

www.BeyondAffairs.com

This couple, who experienced a failed close call, offers a nationwide cluster of support groups, seminars, personal consulting, and various printed materials. On the homepage, you will also find a tab leading to an international listing of the BAN (Beyond Affairs Network) support groups.

www.SmartMarriages.com

This is the "granddaddy" resource for everything you've always wanted to know about marriages, infidelity, close calls, and much more. Established by Diane Sollee, former president of the American Association for Marital and Family Therapists, this Web site and the annual conference focus on "take home and do" resources and have something for everyone interested in marriage.

www.loversforlife-media.com

The Ultimate Relationship Program, Anthony Robbins and Chloe Madanes. Here are ten steps, done in ten days, to transform your love relationship. Includes CDs for each day, a set of follow-up DVDs and the Action Book designed to help you put into practice what you have been viewing. *Close Calls* is a part of this exceptional resource.

BOOKS

Avoiding the Greener Grass Syndrome

Nancy C. Anderson. Grand Rapids: Kregel, 2004. A brief, easy read with lots of practical suggestions that this couple has used to restore their marriage after her affair.

Desperate Marriages

Gary Chapman. Chicago: Northfield, 2008. An updated and revised book formerly titled *Loving Solutions*, this book offers practical help for difficult situations in marriages, including unfaithfulness.

The Five Languages of Apology: How to Experience Healing in All Your Relationships

Gary Chapman and Jennifer Thomas. Chicago: Northfield, 2006. Did you know that sometimes saying "I'm sorry" just isn't enough? Learn how to give and receive meaningful and sincere apologies.

My Husband's Affair Became the Best Thing That Ever Happened to Me

Anne and Brian Bercht. Victoria, British Columbia: Tadford Publishing, 2004. This is the story of a couple who appeared on *Oprah*. Besides telling their personal journey, there are a number of helpful suggestions and resources to protect marriages. Anne also offers personal telephone consultations regarding affairs, inappropriate emotional friendships, and so on.

Not Just Friends

Shirley P. Glass, PhD. New York: The Free Press, 2003. This is the best-researched book available on the topic of close calls. Dr. Glass presented around the world and was on numerous radio and television talk shows until her death in 2005.

Unfaithful: Rebuilding Trust after Infidelity

Gary and Monica Shriver. Colorado Springs: Cook Communications, 2005. After a series of failed close calls and Gary's disclosure of his affairs, he and Monica set about repairing their broken marriage. The lessons they learned and the practices they have put in place to protect their relationship form the core of this material.

MARRIAGE INTENSIVES

Though there are number of these resources around the country, I like the following two options the best. Most marital intensives offer four to eight days of intensive counseling for marriages that need support, healing, love, rest, and major changes in the spousal interactions. The good ones provide quality on-site housing, outstanding meals, wonderful environments, and multiple credentialed therapists. The top programs also have ongoing outcome studies to document their effectiveness. Beware of discount programs. The quality and costs of these two programs, their outcome studies, and their Christian orientation set the benchmark from which to evaluate other offerings.

www.MarbleRetreat.org

Just outside of Aspen, Colorado, this eight-day program was started almost thirty years ago by Dr. and Mrs. Lewis McBurney. Marble Retreat has had a long and fruitful history with multiple denominational leaders and only recently has opened up its services to the entire Christian population, both married and single.

www.NationalMarriage.com

This organization started by Dr. Gary Smalley (and its accompanying Web site) offers several programs for couples. I like the Couples Intensive Program offered in Rome, Georgia. This thirty-hour, four-day program is specifically designed for couples who feel stuck and hopeless in their relationship.

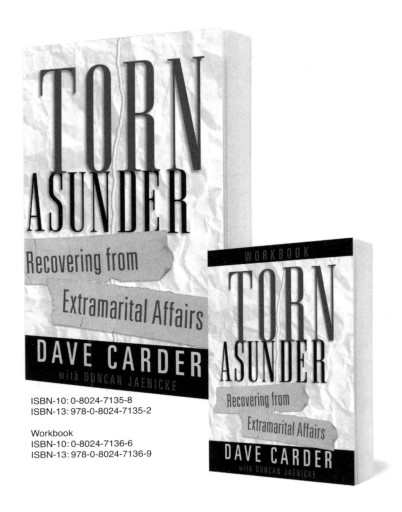

ISBN-10: 0-8024-7135-8
ISBN-13: 978-0-8024-7135-2

Workbook
ISBN-10: 0-8024-7136-6
ISBN-13: 978-0-8024-7136-9

Infidelity is at crisis level even within the church. No marriage is immune, despite apparent moral convictions. Dave Carder wrote *Torn Asunder* to offer couples hope, healing, and encouragement in the face of adultery. He divides his book into first helping readers understand extramarital affairs and then offering healing for marriages dealing with this betrayal. Excellent resource for pastors and leaders, too.

by Dave Carder
Find it now at your favorite local or online bookstore.
www.MoodyPublishers.com